Praise for
Tactics

"Fred,...you've done it again, my friend! Thanks for writing such a powerful and relevant book that addresses the real, tough issues standing in the way of purity. I am just one of many young women grateful to God for using you so profoundly in equipping men of character and integrity. You've not only encouraged the guys but gals like me waiting for their 'holy hunk'!"

—REBECCA ST. JAMES, recording artist and best-selling author

"In the warfare being waged by those who seek to withstand temptation or over-come bondage in the arena of rampant darkness surrounding sexual issues, *Tactics* is a resource that will aid or rescue many."

—DR. JACK W. HAYFORD, chancellor, The King's College and
Seminary, and founding pastor, The Church on the Way

"My good friend Fred Stoeker has crafted the weapons and given you a battle plan to protect and guard your heart as well as restore moral purity when you've fallen. All of Stoeker's books will be must-reads between this grandpa and his grandsons in building godliness and preparing my boys for the good fight."

—DR. GARY ROSBERG, president of America's Family Coaches
and author of *The 5 Sex Needs of Men and Women* and
Divorce-Proof Your Marriage

"*Tactics* hits the issues head-on and helps young men understand how inno-cent actions turn into addiction. With porn available on iPods and lust-driven online social sites like Myspace and Facebook, Fred gives real tools that can help any guy win this important battle."

—BRANDON COTTER, CEO and founder, PureOnline.com

D1024120

"*Tactics* is a brilliant addition to the groundbreaking *Every Young Man's Battle*—insightful and practical as it dismantles lies and shame. A gift of freedom and truth."

> —JOHN and LISA BEVERE, cofounders of Messenger International
> and authors of *A Heart Ablaze* and *Kissed the Girls and Made
> Them Cry*

"Engaging in a topic so many people are afraid to talk about, *Tactics* takes us into the locker room and shows us the playbook, pointing out the opponent's strengths, challenging us to continue to train hard, and reminding us that we have a loving Father who shows up at every game, cheering us on. Fred is the father many of my generation wish they'd had. His words on sexual purity—the specific damage and rewards to one's social life when one radically commits to it—are some of the most insightful I've come across."

> —GLENN LAVENDER and JEREMY THIESSEN, members
> of the Dove Award–winning band Downhere

tactics

Securing the Victory in Every Young Man's Battle

Fred Stoeker with Mike Yorkey

WATERBROOK
PRESS

TACTICS
PUBLISHED BY WATERBROOK PRESS
12265 Oracle Boulevard, Suite 200
Colorado Springs, Colorado 80921
A division of Random House Inc.

10-Digit ISBN: 1-4000-7108-9
13-Digit ISBN: 978-1-4000-7108-1

Library of Congress Cataloging-in-Publication Data
Stoeker, Fred.
   Tactics : securing the victory in every young man's battle / Fred Stoeker with Mike Yorkey. — 1st ed.
       p. cm.
   Includes bibliographical references (p.   ).
   ISBN 1-4000-7108-9
   1. Young men—Religious life. 2. Sex—Religious aspects—Christianity. 3. Masturbation—Religious aspects—Christianity. 4. Chastity. I. Yorkey, Mike. II. Title.
   BV4541.3.S76 2006
   241'.66—dc22

                              2006008985

Printed in the United States of America
2006—First Edition

10 9 8 7 6 5 4 3 2 1

To my heavenly Father

There's no one like You, and I know that You, alone, are God.
But most of all, I know that You are my Abba.

To my sons, Jasen and Michael

You are bright stars in the darkness, real men playing for an audience of One.
I'm glad you've stepped up to join me in our destiny as father and sons.
You are my brothers in Christ, and we will stand.

Contents

Section 5—Experiencing Your Father

Section 6—A Warrior's Challenge

Acknowledgments

Thanks to my dear friend Mike Yorkey; God has been with us from the first day you read my garbled early work in *Every Man's Battle*. You bravely offered to come alongside me, even though *your* only guarantee was the hope God had placed in *my* heart. That took guts. You are a real man.

Thanks to Steve Cobb, Bruce Nygren, and the whole WaterBrook Press team for your awesome skills and your family feel. I love being part of the family!

Thanks to Scott Bruzek and Dave Millis, two of the toughest men I know. Thanks to Mark Oberbeck, Heath Adamson, Gary Meyer, and Dave Roe. Just the sight of you encourages me.

Thanks to Gary Rosberg, who freely pours his heart into mine while knowing full well there is no return in it for him. I don't understand such kindness and grace. Thanks for being you.

Thanks to Lt. Vicky Cluney and Pastor Ray and Joyce Henderson for your ceaseless prayer for my ministry, and thanks to Pastor Dave Olson for gathering the men to pray for me. Thank you, Joel Budd, for shepherding my heart so well for so long from so far away, and special, eternal thanks goes to Pastor Rodger and Liz Sieh and the intercessors in Reinbeck, Iowa. The whole Every Man series was carried into the spiritual darkness of this age upon the shoulders of you, my intercessors. Now, you've carried *Tactics* into the fray. You're off the main highway and plowing the back forty of this world, but the angels know you well. They clasp their hands over their mouths in awe at your faithful response to God's grace.

Gwen Hulett, you've been the mother-in-law of my dreams. You've never once chosen Brenda's side over mine simply because she's your child and I'm not…how many sons-in-law can say that? Your integrity shines brightly, and your love for me is downright inexplicable. I'm surely unworthy, but I'll surely take it.

Blessings to my children: Jasen, Laura, Rebecca, and Michael. The stories of your lives are the stuff of legend to me, and the legend just keeps growing. You guys never change. I couldn't be more grateful for you, and I couldn't enjoy you more as friends. I marvel at your courage, and I marvel at how you *still* think I'm the funniest dad who ever walked the earth.

To my wife, Brenda, your mother's lingering health issues took you into such dark valleys that I wondered if I'd ever be able to find you again. You were sifted like wheat, but we prayed and you sought His face like never before. As usual, your spiritual growth has been nothing short of spectacular, and you are still getting lovelier all the time, in spite of it all. Before I met you, I never saw anything around me that suggested marriage could be this wonderful—every year with you is sweeter than the year before. Your smile captured me years ago, and I'm still just as helplessly yours!

EMBRACING DEFEAT

Searching for the Merle Hay Moment

It's two o'clock in the morning, and you've been wandering aimlessly around campus after giving in for the umpteenth time in your dorm bathroom. You had cleaned up quickly before swinging by your dorm room to grab your copy of *Every Young Man's Battle*. Disgusted with yourself, you then stormed out into the night, too wired to sleep.

Now you've meandered your way into the quad, where you dip your hands in the founder's fountain and scrub them again in anger. Slumping down on the fountain's edge, you lean back and stare absently into the moonlit sky. *How did things ever get this crazy?*

Glancing down at *Every Young Man's Battle*, you suppress a wry grin. At one time the choking chains of sexual sin convinced you that Satan had your number and you'd always be helpless before his onslaughts. After reading the book, though, you believed that you—yes, even you—would become a lust-fighting machine and win this battle within six weeks tops.

But four months have passed, and now you don't know what to think. *What's wrong with me? Joe hasn't masturbated in months, and he says he looks at girls totally differently now.* As for you, all you're seeing are breasts and jeans riding suggestively low. *How exactly do I bounce my eyes from that?*

Actually, you know how—or at least you thought you did after reading *Every Young Man's Battle*. What I said made sense. You did well with your eyes at first, but there were still some difficult things to deal with, like masturbation. You were game anyway. You still remember the thrill of going ten days without doing it, and then working up to twelve. But since then, you've had nothing but trouble. Your eyes haven't bounced as they once did, and sexual thoughts are driving you crazy. Now you're back to masturbating every day or so.

Underneath the dim light of a nearby streetlight, you flip open my book and find yourself comforted by these words:

> God's love is not based upon your ability to meet His standards. God's love for you is unconditional; it never changes. Before you were formed in the womb, He loved you. You're the apple of His eye. His love for you has no limits, and His love for you never wanes. If you masturbate, that fact doesn't lessen your value to Him. If you get up under a girl's bra, God doesn't regret having sent His Son to die for you.

You *know* He can't love you less than He did *before* you were saved. But as you blow a painful sigh into the night, you can't hide the fact that you haven't connected with the Lord very well lately. And you know why, even as my words in the next paragraph grip your heart:

> I recall how the Holy Spirit whispered to me, "This practice can't be tolerated anymore in your life. You are Christ's now, and He loves you." The implication was that continued sexual activity would hurt my intimacy with Christ.
>
> When you break His standards, the Lord doesn't reject you, but you can't be as close to Him. Soon after I prayed that prayer in my office, God told me *No more* in regard to my sexual exploits. Did I feel as though I'd taken an elbow to the chops? Yes. But by the grace of God, I didn't say, *Hey, what's the deal? You're taking my freedom away! You're*

killing me! Instead, I said, *You got it, Father.* This new life in me was moving me His way. I had a desire to be closer to Him. And in order to get closer to Him, I had to be not so close to those women in my life.

"Or too close to the video stores," you mutter. You never realized how much your social life revolved around movies until you read *Every Young Man's Battle* and tried to live purely. You wanted to "starve the sumo" but not your social life.

Tonight it was *Kill Bill* that killed you. The guys said it was okay to watch and not that bad. Still, you were going to duck out until your roommate Garrett teased, "Yeah, and where do you think *you're* going? Quit being so legalistic and sit down with us, you nerd."

You didn't have a good excuse, so you plopped down in the cramped dorm room with Garrett and a couple of buddies. Just as you expected, the movie *was* bad, and the rest of the night you just couldn't get hot Uma Thurman off your mind.

When everyone left long after midnight, you and Garrett turned in, but even after an hour of tossing and turning and staring wide-eyed at the ceiling, you still hadn't fought off those delicious lusts. With that biology exam looming just a few hours away, you couldn't afford another sleepless moment, so you slipped down the hall to release the pressure and put an end to the struggle.

But a lot of peace *that* brought you. Now you're wandering around the campus, and the cool, peaceful pattering of this fountain does little to calm your agitated mind. *These movies do this to me every time! When am I finally going to learn?*

Reading on, you can only nod your head in agreement with the next words:

We must choose oneness and intimacy with Christ. We must choose sexual purity. "It is God's will that you should be sanctified: that you should avoid sexual immorality" (1 Thessalonians 4:3).

It's not enough to *seem* or to *feel* Christian. We must *be* Christians in action. We can't expect to practice with the youth band by day and then slide nude under the sheets with the cute keyboardist by night. We can't expect to circle and hold hands in emotional prayer at church by day then wallow in cybersex by night.

When we turn on the computer and masturbate over naked, nameless lovers lying across our screen, we aren't like Christ. We aren't moving toward Him. While His love for us never changes, our intimacy with Him wanes. Distance grows. But when we choose sexual purity and walk in the light, we're one with God's essence. Intimacy grows. True relationship flourishes.

Staring up at the stars, you wonder, *What's He thinking about me?* You feel absolutely horrible after you masturbate, and you can't sense God's presence. *Is there any hope for me?*

You recall that sexy dream about Heather a week ago after the two of you were instant messaging. The dream was so real and exhilarating that you woke up the next morning certain you'd actually gone all the way with her. She's in the same campus ministry with you, but your online discussions always turn suggestive—mostly about the things you'd both like to check off your to-do lists before graduating from college.

Like the time a month ago when you found yourself bored one weekend. You sent an IM to Heather and picked her up for a mocha at Starbucks. Afterward you strolled past the video store next to the coffee shop. "Should we rent a movie?" you asked.

"Sounds like fun!" Heather said with that smile you like.

You were perusing the aisles when you saw the entrance to the adult section—"No One Under Eighteen Permitted."

Heather's eyes turned mischievous. "Wanna check it out?" she asked. "I've always wanted to!"

"Sure," you said, and the two of you smirked as you read jacket covers and made jokes about the impossibly built babes with their come-hither looks.

Later, as you drove her to her apartment, your casual suggestion about "taking a shower together" met no resistance. A half hour later, you were both toweling off—and you had checked off one more box on your to-do list.

Ever since, you can't keep that memory off your mind, and your conversations with Heather are filled with inside jokes—mostly dirty. And you've wondered a lot, *Why am I playing all these games with God and abusing His grace? Why can't I just love and obey Him?*

Well, at least you've quit looking at porn. You wear that fact proudly, like a badge, but with all this other stuff you're heating up over, you know that very little has really changed. Standing up from the fountain, you step briskly on beneath the full moon, rushing away from the questions pounding in your heart. Tears pool in your eyes. *When is this ever going to end?*

When It Becomes an Addiction

I asked that same question—*When is this ever going to end?*—for the longest time before I finally reached what I call my "Merle Hay Moment." If you can identify with the one-step-forward, two-steps-back story of the college guy at the fountain, you may need a Merle Hay Moment to get you moving forward for good.

What is a Merle Hay Moment? It's a moment we all must find—an instant when your love for your Father finally outweighs your love of your sin, a time when you make a final decision for purity and never look back. For me, that happened *four years* after I had become a Christian.

Here's my story: I was driving down Merle Hay Road in Des Moines, Iowa, minding my own business, when she appeared up the road—a beautiful female jogger, her trim body glistening in the late-afternoon sun. I couldn't keep my eyes off her.

Suddenly it hit me. *I failed Him again!* A crushing wave of sorrow swamped my heart. I just couldn't stand my lustful ways any longer. A volcanic rage erupted from my spirit, and in frustration I slammed the steering wheel with both fists. "That's it!" I yelled. "I'm through with this! I'm making a covenant with my eyes. I don't care what it takes, and I don't care if I die trying. It stops here. It stops *here!*"

Man, what a breakthrough moment for me. Things were never the same again, because now I had *engaged* the battle. Nothing would stop me, because I'd finally and truly made a covenant with the Lord not to let my eyes zero in on the bodies of women.

Have you had a Merle Hay Moment yet? Many guys get there instantly upon reading *Every Young Man's Battle*. God's truth is the source of every Merle Hay Moment, and as you read His truth, you can be set free to rise up and win the battle for purity.

If you haven't read *Every Young Man's Battle* yet—or need a refresher class regarding its contents—let me take a moment to recap the highlights, much like Chris Berman racing through the big plays during halftime of ESPN's NFL Monday Night game.

First of all, I began *Every Young Man's Battle* by describing how I got caught up in pornography and having sex with a succession of young women while I was a student at Stanford University. Then I turned my life around by accepting Jesus Christ into my life and asking forgiveness for my sins—sexual and otherwise.

I married Brenda, and while I didn't read porn magazines anymore, I knew I wasn't even close to God's standard of purity. Then God challenged me one day when I read this scripture: "Why do you call me, 'Lord, Lord,' and do not do what I say?" (Luke 6:46).

What exactly did He mean I wasn't doing? It didn't take me long to figure it out:

"But among you there must not be even a hint of sexual immorality" (Ephesians 5:3).

A *hint*? I had much more than a hint of sexual immorality hiding out in my life. My eyes were ravenous heat seekers, searching the horizon, locking on any target with sensual heat:

Young mothers in shorts, leaning over to pull children out of car seats...
Foxy babes wearing tank tops that revealed skimpy bras...
Joggers in spandex, jiggling merrily down the sidewalks...
Smiling secretaries with big busts and low-cut blouses...

It was critical for me to understand that my eyes could draw as much sexual gratification from looking at these things as they used to get from the pages of a skin magazine. All these "looks" increased my sex drive, which made it practically impossible to eliminate sexual sin and masturbation from my life.

What I said in *Every Young Man's Battle* is that your sex drive was created to be fairly manageable during your single years in high school and college, but the more sensuality you draw through your eyes and fantasies, the more you rev your sexual engine into the red zone, making your sex drive more difficult to control. Furthermore, this same visual gratification releases pleasure chemicals into the pleasure centers of your brain, chemicals that are quite addictive and keep you coming back for more and more.

Your sex drive can grow into the size and girth of a sumo wrestler, and "Mr. Sumo Sex Drive" can become monstrous when you feed him all the sexy images found on cable television, videos, the Internet, and in magazines.

Every Young Man's Battle explained how to cut Mr. Sumo Sex Drive down to size by shutting down the flow of sexual food coming through your eyes and mind so that you can get your sex drive back to normal size. You can cut off the flow of addictive chemicals that keep your mind and body aching for more by *conforming* to God's command to flee every hint of sexual immorality.

My book also described how to get this physical side of the battle under control by making a covenant with your eyes (see Job 31:1) not to lust after the opposite sex, and the best way to do that is to learn to "bounce the eyes" whenever a sensual image pops into your line of sight.

Those actions, along with taking your fantasies and thoughts captive in your mind (see 2 Corinthians 10:5), are critical in your battle for purity, and you'll need your own Merle Hay Moment before you're fully ready to engage the battle for purity.

Embrace Those Defeats

Maybe you're not there yet. If so, that's okay, even if you've already read *Every Young's Man Battle*. You see, it's the losing that will finally bring you home to that moment with God. It's that veil of distance from your Father and that crushing pain of having to look at yourself in the mirror after another demoralizing defeat that eventually bring your will in line with His. You must always despise the pain and distance from God that sin causes, but at the same time, you don't run from it. Never hesitate to embrace your defeats in this battle.

Embrace defeats?

What I'm saying is that you must accept, study, and learn from your defeats. After all, the Lord has asked you to *learn* to control your body in a way that is holy and honorable (1 Thessalonians 4:3–4). This learning may or may not take some time. But if it happens to take more time, you must view each defeat as one more step of learning and one more step toward ultimate victory, rather than letting your heart crumble as the Enemy badgers you with his lies.

I learned plenty from my many defeats before I finally hit my spot on Merle Hay Road. I'd made countless decisions to stop the sin, employing useless tactics that I thought would carry the day in my battle. Every one of them backfired.

For instance, I sincerely believed that my willpower, coupled with my personal "psychology of milestones" that I'd conjured up, would finally ward off my lusts. Here's what I did. Each year when I celebrated my birthday, I would say, "Okay, after this birthday I'm never going to masturbate again. I'll be able to look back and say that I never masturbated after the age of twenty-three!"

I knew so little about my sexuality that I actually believed milestone promises would give me the psychological edge I needed to mark the end of my masturbatory road. I solemnly made such promises every birthday, anniversary, Christmas, and New Year's for years, but I broke them all…often within days, sometimes within hours.

Another tactic was my intensive quest to find a point of no return in my masturbatory power chain—that point beyond which my engines would be so far into the red zone that I couldn't keep from masturbating. I actually watched *Porky's*-type movies for as long as I could without masturbating. I thought that if I could find a so-called tipping point, I could reasonably consume a heaping helping of sensual food anytime I wanted, as long as I stayed on the right side of that point.

Of course, things never worked out because there wasn't a point of no return. Oh, there were times I didn't masturbate, but what I didn't realize was that while revving the engines might not result in masturbating at that moment, my mind could recall those hot scenes anytime it wanted, especially when I was on a business trip and the lights went out in the motel room. I just didn't understand my sex drive or that I needed to starve the sumo in me. I wasted a lot of time churning through a colossal hodgepodge of useless tactics. Still, I did learn a lot and began to understand what worked and what didn't.

I'm grateful that my Merle Hay Moment arrived, and that was the catalyst for getting my eyes under control in six weeks. I felt the spiritual oppression lift and the veil of distance from God vanish.

It was an awesome time of many glorious victories, and my relationship with God blossomed and bloomed in wonderful ways. Compared to the years of beating I had already taken, the battle had become mop-up duty, and the rest was like a downhill march.

Emotional Triggers

I still had to deal with some stiff pockets of resistance, though. While my eyes were under control, my mind was hopelessly out of control with fantasies, and while my masturbation habit had been weakened severely by that covenant with my eyes, it took about three more years before I masturbated for the last time—even though I was married and having all the sex I wanted.

Surprised? Don't be. Masturbation, while obviously sexual in nature, is more than a sexual issue. Sure, there are sexual triggers to masturbation, like watching a double feature of *American Pie* and *American Pie 2.* But there are also emotional triggers, like the stress of finals week. Or perhaps your parents divorced and your dad just moved to Seattle, or your first love just dumped you for your best friend five weeks ago. Loneliness can drive you to let it go.

In my estimation, the emotional triggers to masturbate are often stronger than the sexual triggers, meaning that your masturbation habit may actually be more of an emotional addiction than a sexual one. That's why guys can cut the porn and the eye candy and still find themselves addicted to masturbation. (I'll discuss this aspect about masturbation in later chapters.)

The important point is that my defeats during this mop-up time were absolutely critical to my eventual victory. Every loss taught me more about myself, my emotional triggers, and where my defenses were down.

Here's what I mean. While I was in the midst of my battle, I was a twenty-something working in full-time, full-commission sales. That's right, if you don't sell, you don't eat. Nor do your kids. That was a lot of pressure for a young father, and in order to grow my business, I'd often spend extra hours at the office, rushing back after the kids were asleep so I could write proposals for competitive situations. I knew that if I didn't get things right, I'd blow the deal, and many times I found that the pressure got so high I'd masturbate to blow off steam.

I'd writhe in agony before the Lord after every sexual lapse, but through these defeats, I finally figured out that my masturbation habit was related 100 percent to the stress and had little sexual basis at all. Once I understood that, it was a simpler matter to deal with those lapses because I knew where they came from—an emotional dependence upon myself to provide for the family instead of an emotional dependence upon God to take care of us. In short, I had to learn to depend upon God rather than a handful of lotion, and before long, I'd learned enough about prayer and worship to smash this pocket of resistance. As other defeats brought more understanding, more pockets fell. Before long, there was peace on all sides.

You've likely experienced a string of defeats along the way too. If so, then you can identify with this e-mail I received from Mick:

My name is Mick, and I'm twenty-three years old. This is hard for me to write about, so I am going to try to keep it as brief as possible. I read *Every Young Man's Battle* and loved the entire book. I never realized how much sexual immorality controlled my life or affected my walk with Christ.

I started doing real well after reading your book. I made mistakes here and there, but I knew that the mistakes would happen because it's hard to go cold turkey and change right away.

Lately, though, things have gotten a little worse. I'm masturbating and looking at porn more than I used to, and I am doing things with girls I know aren't right. Afterward I feel so guilty and like I am worth nothing. I ask God for forgiveness, but I turn around and do it again.

I don't know where to turn anymore. I feel like I am letting God down and can never return back to Him. Please help me!

Mick's heart really touched mine, because I remember that desperation. I told him so when I wrote back, explaining some important things about the emotional triggers behind dating and masturbation. Then I gently reminded him that in the end it comes down to a decision: are you going to be who you say you are or not? That decision always determines how much you feed the sumo, how much you bounce your eyes, and how hard you go after those emotional triggers behind the habits.

About a month later, I heard from Mick again:

Thanks for replying back to me. You'll be pleased to learn that it's been a month since I have looked at porn or masturbated. I just wanted to thank you again for the hard work you put into your books and seminars. You are a blessing, and may God continue to bless you and your family.

Mick turned defeat into victory! He wasn't enjoying his defeats; they were killing him, as they would any young man trying to stop the masturbation habit. At the same time, as he embraced those defeats, they spawned a deeper commitment in the core of his heart.

Has Mick gained total victory? Time will tell, but if defeat returns, it'll bring him that much closer to victory as long as he embraces his mistakes and is refined through that fire. The apostle Paul says that suffering and defeat will bring Mick more perseverance and character in the fight:

> Not only so, but we also rejoice in our sufferings, because we know
> that suffering produces perseverance; perseverance, character; and char-
> acter, hope. And hope does not disappoint us, because God has poured
> out his love into our hearts by the Holy Spirit, whom he has given us.
> (Romans 5:3–5)

Of course, this whole discussion begs an important question: what is God doing in the midst of all this defeat? We know His eyes go to and fro throughout the earth, looking for someone on whose behalf He can show His power. What happens when His eyes stop on you? Is He frustrated, throwing up His hands in exasperation and snarling, "I'm going somewhere else! This guy is a loser"?

I doubt it very much, because He has a heart for you as a father has for his son. It's like the heart I have for my sons—only much greater, of course. Let's huddle up a moment and take a closer look at how one father—me— viewed his son's defeats so that you can better understand your Father's attitudes toward yours.

For Personal Reflection

1. Do you see any specific ways in which sexual impurity has weakened your connection with God?

2. If you've noticed magazines, television, movies, or classmates triggering sexual thoughts, are you willing to change your habits? How exactly?

3. Would you say that you are currently accepting your defeats and learning from them, or are you ignoring them and avoiding your Father? Give evidence for your answer.

4. Is there a possibility your sexual sin might have some emotional triggers, not just sexual ones? What sort of emotions do you think trigger your sexual response?

5. Do you currently feel that God is frustrated with you, or do you sense His loving arm around you, helping and guiding you?

Owning the Field

P aying admission had never given me more joy. With a wink and a grin, I squeezed Brenda's hand and took a deep breath of cool September air as we made our way to the west side of the stadium. It was a late afternoon in Iowa, a Thursday, and our team in purple and gold stretched across our end of the field, warming up for the biggest football game in nearly two decades... at least in *my* mind. I hadn't looked forward to the start of *any* football season with this much anticipation since my senior year in high school, when I was the starting quarterback on a team with state-championship aspirations.

Now my youngest son, Michael, was making his gridiron debut for the Johnston Middle School eighth-grade football team. The fact that my son was suiting up in shoulder pads and cleats caused my heart to swirl with flashbacks to my playing days and a conversation Michael and I'd had months earlier. It happened as his wrestling season was drawing to a close in March.

"Dad," he began, "I've been thinking about going out for baseball this spring, but the more I've thought about it, I'd rather get a head start on football. Would you show me how to work out in the weightroom? I want to get a lot stronger."

Whoa! Do quarterbacks hate blitzing linebackers? Of course I would help my son! I quickly devised an upper-body plan involving seven weight stations at a nearby fitness center, and I happily joined him to give him a workout buddy. Every other night after dinner, we drove over to the gym and took turns doing three sets of twelve reps on each strength-training machine. Since it was his first year of working with weights, I had Michael start off quite light, but after curling and pressing our way through the stations for five months, he more than doubled the weighted plates he could handle at each station. As for his body, he added many pounds of muscle to his bulky—for his age— five-foot-eight-inch frame.

Frankly, I'd never seen such determination in a young guy; he never quit, never begged off on a workout, and rarely whined. But then again, he had a partner whom he could trust completely, someone who *knew* all this work would make a difference. He knew I'd been where he wanted to go in football, and that was a huge advantage for him.

By midsummer I added running and jumping rope to our regimen, which took our fitness to the next level. When the first football practice rolled around for the Johnston Middle School football team, I said, "Michael, congratulations! Your work is over!"

"What do you mean?" he said, a surprised look on his face. "Practice starts tomorrow! It's the middle of August, and it's really hot out there. Don't you remember what the first week of practice was like for me last year? I thought I'd die every single day!"

"Listen, buddy, no one who's ever donned pads in Iowa can ever forget what August is like," I said. "But now is when your fun starts, just the same. You did the real work during the off-season. That's when champions are made—when no one knows and no one cares if you were working out. But now it's fun time. Now it's time for you to go out and enjoy everything you've worked for."

"Oh, I get it, Dad. I'll try to have fun, but I still don't know if I can even get through it all! Maybe I won't be good enough," Michael said honestly.

"I know you're nervous about practice, but let me clue you in on something. No one else on your team has done what you did to get ready for this

football season, I guarantee you. While your teammates were out playing baseball and going to the movies and playing Madden football on the computer
all summer, you were lifting weights and preparing for this day."

I patted his chest. "All that work is in here, deep down inside, and no one
can take it away from you. You have an edge, and it's too late for any of them
to catch up. That edge will be there when you need it every afternoon, so go
out and have fun. Show them who owns the field, Son."

Going Both Ways

During preseason practice, Michael quickly earned starting spots on both sides
of the ball, at right guard on offense and left tackle on defense. As I predicted,
practice was fun for him, so now, on this lovely late afternoon in September,
it was time for me, his personal trainer, to have a little fun as well.

Brenda and I settled into our seats with our Cokes and cameras to watch
Michael run through his warmups before the big game. I'd worked out at
Michael's side for months and had dreamed of this day with him. I could
hardly contain myself as I waited for the opening kickoff! As the Mason City
team trotted onto their end of the field to warm up, I mused back on what I'd
told Michael the previous night as we drove home from practice.

"Son, I just can't wait for this first game with Mason City," I began. "I
know you'll have the time of your life. Still, there's one thing I need to warn
you about before you take the field tomorrow. You know how you've been
dominating the guys you've been blocking in practice the last few weeks?"

Michael looked at me and nodded.

"Well, it's not going to be quite like that in a real game," I said.

"What do you mean, Dad?" he said, instantly on edge. "I thought you
said I'm really strong."

"You are, Son," I'd continued. "But remember, you've only been blocking
B-team guys in practice so far. When Mason City comes to town, they'll line
up their A-team guys against you both ways."

I smiled at the look on his face. He hadn't yet thought of that.

"You needn't worry, Son," I reassured him. "I just want you to know that on the first snap, you'll be really surprised when you hit the guy across from you. You won't just blow him off the line like you do your teammates in practice. You'll be getting his best shot, an A-team-style shot, but don't be discouraged. Just hit him again on the next snap. Remember, you've got all the strength you need inside."

Momentarily I was lost in my thoughts, but Brenda's tremulous voice soon pierced my ears and snapped me back to the present. "Oh no!" she groaned. "They are *way* bigger than we are, Fred. Look at that number 99 out there. He's huge!"

"Oh, don't worry about him," I reassured her. "Pads will make anyone look huge."

She wasn't buying it. "Can you take a closer look and make sure for me?"

Since I was having trouble sitting still anyway, I took her up on it and sauntered down to Mason City's side of the field for a closer look. Alas, Brenda's suspicions were true. Number 99 *was* huge, and he was already my height. In eighth grade, mind you!

As I headed back to my seat for the opening kickoff, I was glad I had warned Michael about what to expect on that first play from scrimmage, because sure enough, as Michael broke from the huddle for the first play— you guessed it—facing him was big old number 99. At the snap of the ball, the two hit each other like a couple of grizzly bears caught in some epic turf battle on the Discovery Channel. The ground shook, and neither moved the other an inch. Brenda sat petrified, nervously clenching and reclenching my hand, but I honestly wasn't worried. I'd practiced blocking with Michael all summer, and I knew my son was a real load. It didn't matter how tall this kid was; Mr. 99 would have his hands full for all four quarters.

And I was right. Within a few plays, Michael began to get the upper hand, and Mr. 99's body language—revealed through my binoculars—told me that he'd had quite enough of this head-on head banging. Even though our side eventually lost the game, Michael owned that spot of ground over right guard until the final whistle.

At the dinner table that night, I asked, "Hey, Michael, are you glad I warned you about that first snap of the ball and that first hit?"

"*Yes!*" He said it so emphatically we both burst out laughing.

"You'd have been discouraged otherwise, wouldn't you? Man, he was big."

"Dad, I don't know what I'd have done if you hadn't told me about that first snap ahead of time. I *know* I'd have been scared. But because you told me what to expect, I just figured this was normal stuff and that I'd better get going harder."

It's good to know the ropes ahead of time, isn't it? Michael's learning to own the field in football, just as I tried to do when it was my turn to play. I can show him how. I've been where he wants to go.

Distractions

Michael's also fighting to own things on another field of play, an arena where every young man must battle—his sexuality. I'm glad I've run on the same turf as well, and I can show him how to get there too.

Working through our weight stations one June evening at the club, three ponytailed high-school girls suddenly bounced in out of nowhere, giggling and chattering away. They were definitely cute and minimally dressed for their workout. One even wore a "wife beater" T-shirt—one of those thin, tank-style men's cotton undershirts designed to reveal every curve and rippling muscle. Most of the guys scattered about the weightroom couldn't keep their eyes to themselves.

Fortunately, the girls left as abruptly as they'd arrived. The room became quiet again, and Michael and I simply pushed on to the next station without a word about what had just happened. After skipping some rope and taking a quick shower, we straggled across the parking lot, plodding across the lengthening shadows of the lovely trees stretching up beneath a golden Iowan sunset.

Michael, shuffling a half step behind me, ventured, "You know, Dad, it would sure be better if girls weren't allowed into the weightroom with us guys."

"I know what you mean, Son." And I really did. I knew he was talking about the way they were dressed and the pressure it puts on a guy in his battle for purity.

But Michael wasn't sure I'd caught his drift. "It isn't that I don't think girls should be allowed to lift weights. I'm not against girls or anything like that, Dad."

"I know, Son. You were just bothered by what they were wearing."

"That's right! Why do they do that? Don't they understand what that does to us?"

"Well, maybe or maybe not. But you know what I've learned? It really doesn't matter whether they understand. What matters is what we do when they come into the weightroom."

"I looked away, Dad, but they seemed to be everywhere."

"Let me share a trick with you," I said as we stopped walking. "I've found that a guy can use his peripheral vision to keep track of where they are without getting a full view of their bodies and everything, so this is what we'll do. When you're lifting, I'll find out where they are in my peripheral vision, and then I'll turn my back to them slightly and simply watch you while you lift. When I'm lifting, you can do the same thing, and we'll both be fine."

"That sounds great, Dad."

As we jumped into the car and pulled out onto Merle Hay Road, Michael smiled. "Dad, thanks for telling me how to use my peripheral vision in all this. I'd have never thought about that on my own."

I can assure you that Michael was thankful to learn a few things about his sexual field of play, because real game knowledge gives him an edge, just as it does on the gridiron. He wants to own the field.

What about you? Do you own your sexuality, or is your opponent pushing you all over the field? Do you have what it takes to own this patch of turf?

When I played football, I always tried to own the field, whether at home or away. I played as if the turf were mine and I could go wherever I wanted. If anyone dared to try to stop me, he'd get what he deserved—a lowered shoulder and some driving legs.

I knew the sacrifices I'd made to get strong. I knew that I'd outworked everyone else on the field during the months leading up to Friday night, and I promised myself that no one player would ever get the best of me. I belonged on that field, and that field belonged to me. Only the commitment that led to my strength, balance, and confidence mattered out there.

Commitment to Excellence

Commitment also matters on the sexual field of play, but I'm not just talking about your commitment to be disciplined in your obedience to your Coach. I'm also talking about the commitment of your life to Christ that placed a better kind of power inside of you, and you didn't have to lift an ounce in the weightroom to earn it:

> His divine power has given us everything we need for life and godliness
> through our knowledge of him who called us by his own glory and
> goodness. Through these he has given us his very great and precious
> promises, so that through them you may participate in the divine
> nature and escape the corruption in the world caused by evil desires.
> (2 Peter 1:3–4)

Scripture clearly reminds you that you already have everything inside that you need to own this field. Sometimes, though, you get sacked—blindsided out of nowhere. After one jarring A-team hit after another, you know you don't own the field any longer. That's when you hear Satan's trash talk, ripping you for being weak and letting your defenses down. Sometimes the Enemy just looks huge, like big old 99. You begin to wonder if you've got what it takes.

My heart for Michael was touched deeply during the fourth game of the season. After a month of play, Michael had seen plenty on the football field. He had yet to line up against anyone his size or smaller, but on this night it had gotten ridiculous. "Dad," he confessed after this game, "I took a good look through his face mask on the first play and said to myself, *Whoa, this guy is way past puberty.* He was a gorilla! He had hair sprouting out everywhere!"

To Michael, then a thirteen-year-old, playing against someone who needed a shave would mean a long day in the trenches. On nearly every snap of the ball, the gorilla delivered a blow that blew my son back a step. Michael would then dig in and hand fight the beast, holding his ground to contain him, but he could do little else with him. At other times, the gorilla slanted right while a linebacker blitzed through Michael's spot on the line. Sometimes Michael picked up the blitz and stopped it cold. Sometimes he didn't.

It was a long first half. Once the horn blew for halftime, Michael ran to the bench, shaking his head. Grabbing a quick blast of water before heading into the locker room, he sneaked a glance at me, sitting in the stands, to see what I was thinking. I could read the question all over his face: *What are you thinking of me?*

He knew he hadn't owned the field that half. He knew he had missed a few assignments and was hurting from the shots he'd taken. Naturally, he wondered what his father felt about him at that moment.

I'll tell you what I was feeling: I shot him two thumbs-up and a big fat grin. He acknowledged me with a slight wave and a little smile. Okay, he's not Orlando Pace yet, but he's my son, and I'm with him. He loves football. He loves working out with me. He's *learning* how to fight out there on the gridiron.

Am I eager for him to own the field someday? Yes, very much so. Does he need more coaching? Absolutely. Do I think he's a dork or a loser? Not on your life.

Sure, it would be nice if Michael owned the field already, but eighth grade is eighth grade. Ninth grade will be ninth grade. Defeats will come, and he'll play poorly at times. But I want him to embrace those defeats, learn from his mistakes, allow me to sort through them with him, and then move back in to attack again. That's how warriors are born, and that's how a father handles his son's defeats.

Now, what about that Father of yours who's promised that He will work all things together—including your defeats—for your good? Look, He knows His way around this field of purity, and He knows what the battle is like. His Son, Jesus, played on these same fields, and while that Son went undefeated, your Father saw just how vicious the Enemy can be.

He knows this Enemy. He created Satan and his angels eons ago, before they turned against Him, and He has been there every time these demons have wrestled with His sons over the centuries. He knows each of them by name, and as you now step into the ring to take your own turn grappling with them, He knows each malicious trap they'll set for you before your foot even touches the mat.

But the Father also knows one more thing. You're His son, and He'll be with you every moment as you learn how to win. He's there to restore you, and He will embrace defeat with you all day long, because He knows He can use it to restore you, to encourage you, and to help you love Him more.

Total Integration

Remember, this call to purity has always been more about your relationship with God than anything else. That's why we were created, and that's why He sent His Son—that we might walk with God in the garden in the cool of the day, shoulder to shoulder, heart to heart.

Never forget that this call to purity is about much more than stopping masturbation. It's about experiencing God in those moments that would have been dedicated to sex. It's about finding God and His help in the midst of every struggle, every failure, and every frustration. It's not about extinguishing masturbation as much as it's about igniting a new passion for God, with your sexuality integrated into your life in a balanced way. It's about embracing suffering and loss, because defeat deepens that yearning to look Him in the eye again.

If you fail, stop beating yourself up, and, above all, stop listening to the Enemy. God is not mad, throwing up His hands in exasperation. Why would He give up now when you're His child if He didn't give up when you were lost?

> You see, at just the right time, when we were still powerless, Christ died for the ungodly. Very rarely will anyone die for a righteous man, though for a good man someone might possibly dare to die. But God demonstrates his own love for us in this: While we were still sinners, Christ died for us. (Romans 5:6–8)

He's not going anywhere. He's here to restore you, and He simply wants to make you a man after His own heart. He made one of David:

> So [Jesse] sent and had [David] brought in. He was ruddy, with a fine appearance and handsome features.
> Then the LORD said, "Rise and anoint him; he is the one."
> So Samuel took the horn of oil and anointed him in the presence of his brothers, and from that day on the Spirit of the LORD came upon David in power. (1 Samuel 16:12–13)

God wants to make you spiritually handsome and ruddy on the inside. He wants you to be a mighty man fully committed to making Jesus king in your heart. He wants to anoint you in the presence of your brothers, and He wants to come upon you in power. He's not here to raise up nice-looking, obedient little boys with tucked-in shirts and straight parts in their hair. He wants to make you into a mighty man of valor who hates the Enemy's work as He does.

Battles—and especially defeats—test and transform soldiers, and your response to your defeats will reveal the depth of your love for Him. You're stronger, and you're changed. So when you lose, rise up, pray, and hit the ramparts again. With each victory, your spiritual, emotional, and physical attributes will line up a little more with the Lord's.

The good news of the gospel is that it's not just about forgiveness and grace; it's also about full restoration. God doesn't intend to set you free only to leave you hobbling your way home to heaven. Granted, restoration may be instantaneous or may take some time, but it's always "restoration or bust" as far as He is concerned. He'll never stop at forgiveness, because He wants to transform your mind and to enjoy your future with you, together and forever.

How long will this take for you? I don't know, but that isn't the important question to God, or to any other normal father, for that matter. For example, the level of Michael's *commitment* to football is far more important to me than how long it'll take him to own the field, and I believe the same is true with your heavenly Father. That means the far more pertinent questions—and their answers—would be these:

- Have you fully engaged the battle?
- Does your heart fully agree that you have no right to live any way other than the way Jesus lived?
- Are you ready to win or die trying, no matter what anyone else thinks about you?

Once you can say yes to all three of these questions, the time frame becomes irrelevant to Him. You will own the sexual field of play soon, and that's good enough for God.

Look, He knows it can take some time, because He knows that purity is a confusing game. After all, there are two fronts to this battle. To win the battle for purity, you must develop an effective, practical strategy for engaging the Enemy on both fronts: the spiritual front (running closer to God and your brothers in Christ) and the physical front (fleeing sensual pollution). As I said, I devoted most of the pages in *Every Young Man's Battle* to the physical front of this battle, teaching what it looks like to "flee" sexual immorality—bouncing the eyes, starving the sumo, taking thoughts captive.

If you are still losing, you may need some more coaching in this physical arena, which I'll give to you in the first few chapters of *Tactics*. Winning on this front is absolutely critical and is often the key break in the game, as this e-mail attests:

I used to be full of lust and perverted sexual tendencies, but through God's Word and *Every Young Man's Battle,* I have been set free! It really is possible to make a covenant with your eyes and not drool over a woman that walks by.

Making this covenant on the physical front may turn the tide of the battle completely in your favor, just as it did in my life. But even if it does just that, don't stop there. Get up and fight and win on the spiritual front too. Remember, we don't flee immorality just to stop the drooling. We flee to find our way back into our Father's arms. We flee for the intimacy, to be satisfied in Him alone.

You'll find this kind of intimacy and satisfaction only by winning on the spiritual front of the battle. So even if you've already read *Every Young Man's Battle* and you feel that you're doing well bouncing your eyes and starving the sumo, you'll still want to finish *Tactics* and engage the Enemy on the spiritual front too. Victory there can cement your victories into place permanently.

You see, while the physical part is about *conforming* to God's direction in His Word, the spiritual part is more about *transforming* your sexually driven mind into the mind of Christ through His power.

In short, you must own both ends of the playing field to establish total victory. That's why I strongly suggest you read *Every Young Man's Battle* if you haven't done so; you'll need its defensive schemes to protect your end of the field. But since I barely touched on the spiritual front of the battle in that book, you may also need the tactical help from *Tactics* in the areas of prayer, worship, and Bible study to increase your passion for the Lord on the offensive end.

Intimacy with God brings a complete transformation of your mind and heart toward purity. God wants to give you real game knowledge so you'll have an edge on this sexual field of play. Most of all, He wants you to know you've got what it takes in your heart. He placed that new life inside you, remember? You have an edge inside, and it'll be there when you need it. So He's not a bit concerned as He watches you line up against your Enemy. He knows the Enemy will have his hands full the whole game, and your Father's just dying to see your next play. It's time to make the push, so tighten your chin strap and take the field.

Enemy Obstacles

As you hit the field once more, what obstacles may be blocking you from total victory? Or, asked another way, on which front of the battle are you stumbling? As I said, it may be that you simply haven't engaged the battle effectively on the *spiritual* side of things yet. If so, I'm anxious to get to that end of the field and devise some strategy with you. I'll do that with you in section 3 of this book.

But it could also be that you still haven't effectively engaged things on the *physical* side of the battle, in spite of everything you learned from *Every Young Man's Battle*. To win on the physical front, your objective is easily defined—you must discipline yourself to guard your eyes, mind, and heart from the sensual pollution around you. If you are still losing today, you may have undetected cracks in your defenses, and too much sensual sewage may be leaking in unnoticed through your eyes.

Before I address the tactics you'll need to win on the spiritual front of the battle, let's drop back and take another close look at the carnage caused by the lust of the eyes and the addictive patterns that can settle into your sexuality.

For Personal Reflection

1. In terms of inner strength, what are a few ways that a commitment to Christ is similar to a commitment to weight training?
2. How does a loving father react to his son's defeat?
3. True or false: Your heavenly Father understands that sexual purity is a learning process that can take time. (See 1 Thessalonians 4:3–8.)

4. Ponder the questions on page 27: Have you fully engaged the battle? Do you fully agree in your heart that you have no right to live any way other than the way Jesus lived? Are you ready to win over your flesh, no matter what anyone else thinks about you?

5. If you are still losing your battle for purity, what are the two most influential temptations?

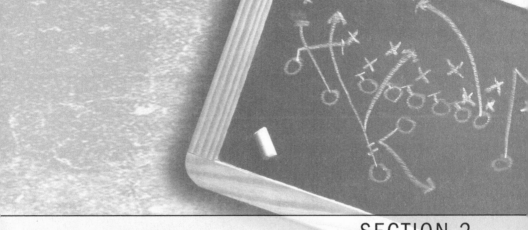

THE PHYSICAL FRONT OF THE BATTLE

Searching for Normal

Eye Damage

If you don't own the field yet, you are likely confused and demoralized, asking, "What's wrong with me? Why am I such a sissy in this battle?" You may even doubt the truth by now, wondering, "How pure can a guy really be anyway?"

Maybe you've managed to get 80 percent there, but you can't quite push things over the top for total victory. You're thinking, *Why have I been able to quit the porn but not the masturbation?* That was John's question:

> I was saved when I was twelve but got serious about God when I was sixteen. Unfortunately, my curiosity led me to get hooked on pornography during those years in between. Thankfully, after getting very close to having intercourse with my girlfriend, I committed my heart completely to God and haven't touched porn since. But in spite of that, masturbation has become a seemingly unbreakable habit for me. I read *Every Young Man's Battle* and made a firm decision to stop, but within three weeks, I gave in again. Now I'm starting to fall more often, and it's making me feel like God is so far away.

Perhaps you *were* free, but now you've got a girlfriend and you're pushing the boundaries with her—even though you thought you had that sexual purity thing settled once and for all. Steve wonders where the victory went:

> I read *Every Young Man's Battle* and got my sexual life under control. In the months that followed, I grew close to God, closer than I'd ever been. I was ecstatic when I met Amber, excited to have the chance to honor a girl with my sexuality for a change. I wasn't the least bit worried about my purity since I thought that having a steady girlfriend would make the battle go even easier. After all, we would be strengthening each other and growing closer to God together, right?
>
> But that's not what happened. Dating only made the battle worse. Then, after our breakup, I struggled even more with impure thoughts, which killed me, because now I was right back where I started.

What *is* up with all these partial victories? We are Christians. Again, Scripture reminds us that we already have everything we need to own this field:

> For His divine power has bestowed upon us all things that [are requisite and suited] to life and godliness, through the [full, personal] knowledge of Him Who called us by and to His own glory and excellence (virtue). By means of these He has bestowed on us His precious and exceedingly great promises, so that through them you may escape [by flight] from the moral decay (rottenness and corruption) that is in the world because of covetousness (lust and greed), and become sharers (partakers) of the divine nature. (2 Peter 1:3–4, AMP)

If that's so, then why don't we own the field already?

Let's return to Michael's first football game for a little insight into that question. I told Michael that lifting weights during the spring and summer had given him everything he needed inside to win and that it would all be there when he needed it. And it was. He owned his spot on the line the entire game.

Still, while that was a great start, it only took him part of the way. Michael may have had more strength than he'd ever had before, but he needed some tactical help if he was going to become a dominant presence on the gridiron. Michael could jeopardize his strength advantage by taking the wrong angle on a running back or getting sucked in on a fake—breaking containment. He could stop early on his blocks, allowing the opponent to slip off and make a tackle. He could pull out on a counter play as the lead blocker, but if he didn't hit the right defender as he turned up the hole, everything would spill into chaos. Without these tactical skills, Michael was never going to own the whole field in football.

And without the tactical skills to fight every young man's battle, you may never get to where you want to go in your purity, either. Like Michael, you already have all the strength you'll need to own the field because of Christ's new life living inside you, but perhaps you are still doing things that compromise that strength. The game-speed chaos in your relationships with girls may be rocking your senses, but is it the smaller, under-the-radar things that are doing you in?

On the sexual field of play, most of the things that compromise your inner strength sneak up on you from the outside without notice, as they did with Kirk:

Before then, I would have categorized myself as a casual observer of porn. But after watching your video, I realized that I was more addicted to the stuff than I previously thought. When I tried to quit the habit completely, I found I couldn't. It just never occurred to me that consuming porn could be addictive to a normal guy like me.

Guys don't like to hear that their "innocent" porn habit could be an addiction, but that's the right word. When you think of "porn" and "addiction," you might picture something dark and seedy and therefore relegate the whole notion to some sick guys in need of serious psychological help. But the true experts on the effects of pornography use say there's a six-step progression that takes place when someone uses porn:

1. Early exposure
2. Addiction
3. Voyeurism and the objectification of women
4. Escalation
5. Desensitization
6. Acting out sexually

Whoa, that could never be me! you think.

Hey, I felt the same way back in college. I wasn't addicted to porn, even though I committed to memory the date each month that my favorite skin magazine, *Gallery,* arrived at the local drugstore. I couldn't be a voyeur, even though my favorite section in *Gallery* was "Girls Next Door," where guys sent in snapshots of their naked girlfriends for the rest of the world to see. I couldn't be desensitized sexually, even though I was making sure that my bed was well supplied with one nubile and willing woman after another. *What's abnormal about any of that?*

Besides, I was way too smart and cool to be addicted. I was a Stanford student, well on my way in life. If you had asked me back then about porn and addiction, I would have told you to save your breath for those drooling guys who need shrinks to deal with their problems.

Twenty-five years later, I know better. The fact is, most young men in America are exhibiting the first three patterns of addiction simply because they've grown up in a sensualized American culture, and if they are using porn, they've tacked on one or two more points from the addiction progression list, whether they recognize it or not.

Porn is so potent that you don't need an "underlying psychological disorder" to fall into these patterns. You just need to be male. A guy receives a chemical high from sexually charged images, because a hormone called epinephrine is secreted into the bloodstream. The result: whatever stimulus present at the time of the emotional excitement is locked into memory. Because of this, the average guy experiences the same kinds of chemical highs and sexual gratification that a full-blown sex addict craves.

Now, it *is* still possible to spot this addictive sequence in your life, even though you're used to living with the damages caused by porn and even though the scientific lingo can throw you off. Let me shed some light—through an MRI of sorts—onto what those fancy-sounding six steps of addiction look like in everyday life.

Phase 1: Early Exposure

Most guys who get addicted to porn start early. They see the stuff when they are very young, and it grabs them by the ankles and doesn't let go. My eyeballs popped huge in first grade when I found a *Playboy* magazine under my father's bed. My situation wasn't unusual: 50 percent of American boys catch their first glance of porn before the age of eleven. I expect that age to fall even further as "porn shots" become widely available on cell-phone screens.

But if we're honest, we don't even need this tsunami of digital technology to get an early exposure to tantalizing images of the female form. All we need is a casual stroll through a good old-fashioned American mall. I was reminded of this a couple of years ago after my son Michael returned from a shopping trip. Brenda took him and his three siblings to a nearby mall one wintry Saturday morning while I stayed behind to jam on some writing.

They returned in the afternoon lugging large, lumpy shopping bags. From my basement office I could hear them making a ruckus upstairs, so I made a mental note to find a stopping point and go check out all the excitement.

Meanwhile, Michael—eleven years old at the time—sneaked up behind his mom and wrapped his short arms around her waist. Brenda turned around with a smile, only to discover a pair of searching eyes leveled upon hers. "Mom, how do you get pictures of women in their underwear out of your head?" he implored.

Brenda, to her credit, kept smiling, but inside she wondered if she had heard her son correctly. When she realized she had, she didn't miss a beat.

"Why don't you go ask your father that question?" she said, tousling his hair and pointing him toward the basement. "But before you go, exactly what kind of pictures are you talking about?"

"Remember when we walked to the food court for lunch today?"

"Sure."

"Well, when we walked past that 'secret store,' I saw all those women in the window wearing that underwear. I haven't been able to get those pictures out of my head all day."

Suddenly everything clicked for Brenda—and for me when Michael told me what had happened. That "secret store" was Victoria's Secret, the intimate apparel emporium with the lifelike mannequins in suggestive poses wearing lingerie. Perhaps consciously for the first time, Michael had experienced the ability of male eyes to chemically lock in such sensual images with only a glance.

Thankfully, I helped Michael sort out his interesting afternoon in the mall. But for other boys, what if a father isn't there? Every young man's battlefield has been dramatically altered by the nuclear sexual blasts of the Internet and MTV, and soon the wireless, pornographic carpet bombing of cell phones will shell the landscape beyond recognition. Early exposure is practically a given.

Phase 2: Addiction

Without parental guidance, early exposure to porn practically guarantees a move to this second phase of damage, as Tom can easily attest:

> When I was eleven, our teacher discussed masturbation in our sixth-
> grade sex ed class. Naturally curious, I went home to try it out, and I
> was hooked. That quickly led me into pornography, which choked me
> for the next fifteen years. I could go a week without it, sometimes two,

but I couldn't kick it and always ended up in the same place, doomed
to failure.

Porn has a way of becoming a regular part of your life. When you get
hooked, it's hard to wiggle free. The "experts" riding on your school bus or
residing in your dorms won't admit that you can get hooked, because they
didn't hear anything about that in their middle-school sex ed class.

But at a recent U.S. Senate hearing regarding whether porn is a form of
free speech deserving protection by the First Amendment, psychiatrist Jeffrey
Satinover testified regarding pornography's effect on brain chemistry. Satinover stated that it was time to quit regarding porn as just another form of artis-
tic expression. "[Porn] is a very carefully designed delivery system for evoking
a tremendous flood within the brain of endogenous opioids," he said. "Mod-
ern science allows us to understand that the underlying nature of an addiction
to pornography is chemically nearly identical to a heroin addiction."

Many of the most powerful chemicals in the human body are involved in
and around orgasm, including dopamine, which produces a pleasurable effect
in the brain that some have estimated to be thirty times more powerful than
cocaine, according to an addictions counselor I spoke to. That pleasure makes
it hard to stop once you get hooked on porn, as Terry described to me:

> When I became a Christian, I quit fooling around sexually with girls. I
> quit cold turkey. I stopped drugs, quit swearing, and stopped smoking
> and drinking. I turned my life around, to Him be the honor and the
> glory. The only thing I couldn't kick was the porn. I tried and tried and
> tried to kick it on my own, but every time I screwed up, I cried and
> promised myself I would never screw up again—until the next day.

Phase 3: Voyeurism and the Objectification of Women

Porn's toxic cascade soon causes you to "objectify" women. A lot of guys don't
know what that means. I had one fellow post this message to the board at Iowa

State University: "What the heck does objectify mean? That's a term that gets thrown around a lot but seems to have no meaning. I don't treat women as objects just because I've seen porn, so how can you say it causes objectification?"

How does he know he doesn't objectify women if he doesn't even know what it means? While it's easy to be confused by such scientific jargon, I'd bet the farm he'd see a lot of "objectifying" in his behavior once he realized what it looks like in real life, which Brandon's story demonstrates:

> I'm a newly married man and had a problem looking at women and some Internet porn on occasion. But it was the everyday looking and admiring the bodies of ladies at work, on the public transit, and in the marketplace that caused me to compare my wife to other women and to see women as sex objects. I really think more men have a problem with this than we realize. It seems so harmless because you rationalize, *There's nothing wrong with this... I'm not even talking to these women!*

Once we begin to objectify women, it's like there's a constant, low hum of their sexuality buzzing around our heads when we're around them. Troy's story illustrates it well:

> Despite the fact that I've had a girlfriend for eighteen months now, I generally look forward to my long plane flights back and forth from college in hopes that I might sit next to an attractive young girl so I can try to get my "swerve on." If she flirts with me, that's confirmation that I'm attractive enough for her to show interest. When that happens, I allow my mind to entertain thoughts of various sexual acts with this young woman.
>
> I've been looking at porn and masturbating since I was thirteen, and since puberty, I really haven't lived life without it. My biggest problem now is that I find it very difficult to just look at a girl and not think about us having sex. I'm not interested in dating them—just hav-

ing sex with them. I even think about that with the pure, decent ones. It can be any girl between the ages of fifteen and twenty-five. If they look good, I'm thinking about sex with them.

Do you see how porn warps the way you look at young women? Girls do not take off their tops and jump into bed with you the minute they meet you. But that's the lie that porn sells, along with the idea that when girls say no, they really mean yes. Compared to your drool sessions on the Internet, of course, your day-to-day lustful thoughts may *seem* more innocent and subtle when you're sitting on an airplane or flirting with some girl at the student union. But the bottom line is that porn has changed how you view women.

Voyeurism also becomes your problem. I heard of one of its latest mutations from Henry J. Rogers, author of *The Silent War: Ministering to Those Trapped in the Deception of Pornography,* as he spoke on Gary Rosberg's *America's Family Coaches* radio program. "There are guys in crowded school hallways who put their cell phones underneath girls' skirts and take pictures," Rogers said. "You get a girl wearing a short skirt, walking up the stairs in a high-school building, and it's not a difficult thing to do."

Taking pictures like this with a cell phone is a form of voyeurism. What's a voyeur? A fancy French word for a Peeping Tom, who in the days before cell phones would peek through bedroom windows while a couple was having sex or through a bathroom window after a woman hopped out of the shower.

Voyeurism isn't limited to peepholes and peep shows, however. Thinking more broadly, voyeurism is that tendency to want to look at women rather than interact with them, to enjoy their bodies while ignoring the psychological and emotional aspects of a healthy, personal relationship.

Sometimes you participate in voyeuristic behavior without trying. It nearly happened to me on a trip home from Dallas, where I'd been teaching a weekend men's retreat on sexual purity. On this occasion, I boarded the plane and took an aisle seat. As I rested my elbow on the armrest and lay my head on my hand, my eyes focused aimlessly ahead as my fellow passengers filtered by. I was exhausted, and I hoped my seatmate would arrive quickly so I could stand up one last time before grabbing forty winks.

Presently, a young woman caught my eye with a faint smile and nodded toward the window seat, which was next to mine. I stood up politely to let her squeeze in, and then I settled down to buckle in. About ten minutes after take-off, I absent-mindedly glanced out the window at the billowing clouds. As I did, I noticed this young woman had already laid her head back to sleep, and her low-cut top was offering a feast for my eyes.

Was I tempted? Nah. I simply turned the other way. At this point in my life, a lingering peek down a woman's blouse wasn't going to happen. I'm not "in" to body-part comparisons anymore. Regarding the pretty young woman sitting next to me, I had settled in my mind years ago how I would respond.

But as I closed my eyes, I pondered what could have happened at one time. My eyes would have roamed all over her, using her body for my selfish pleasure without her consent. *And even worse,* I mused, *I'd have been using her without her knowledge!*

Suddenly it hit me: peeking down her top as she slept beside me would have been no different than, say, using a telescope to watch her undress through her bedroom window. Christian men are adopted sons of the Most High God. We shouldn't take part in such degrading behavior. And yet many Christian men engage in voyeurism all the time—at the movie theater. Watching sex-drenched PG-13 and R-rated movies is voyeurism. In God's eyes, there is little difference between your watching others have sex on the screen in the padded comfort of your family room and your having sex with the deacon's daughter in the padded comfort of the backseat of your car. Both are sin.

Phase 4: Escalation

After a while, things escalate with porn, as this e-mail from Matt demonstrates:

> I started masturbating when I was twelve, the year I got "the talk" from my dad. Then I started getting more active online. I loved gaming

forums, especially my favorite game—Starfox. Eventually, somebody popped up a comic about Starfox. I checked it out, but it wasn't sexual or anything. Then I looked at the mother site...wow! I scrolled through sexual drawings by the dozens, and after a while, you can guess what I did while I looked. After that, I started looking for more porn sites. Then, with my natural ability as a writer, I even wrote sex stories, which I posted for other people to enjoy.

You could say that Matt's addiction escalated when he searched for more graphic porn after comic porn no longer turned his crank, but it's not because he has some "fixation" or "disorder." Like the other binding links in this addictive chain, escalation is a natural step of the progression simply because of the way your eyes and your sexuality were created.

In fact, escalation happens so easily that you usually don't notice you're ratcheting things up. In her testimony before the U.S. Senate, Dr. Mary Anne Layden of the University of Pennsylvania said, "Sexual addicts develop tolerance and will need more and harder kinds of pornographic material. They have escalating compulsive sexual behavior—becoming more out of control—and also experience withdrawal symptoms if they stop the use of the sexual material."

In other words, when you get immersed in online porn, you'll go places you never would have dreamed of going before you were hooked. That's what happened to Brady:

I'm a twenty-one-year-old Christian college student, and I don't know why I feel compelled to tell you this, but maybe I just need to get if off my chest. The sad thing is not just that I'm hooked on regular porn, but now I'm into homosexual porn. I hate myself for this. I'm still attracted to women in porn, but it's usually in a completely degrading way.

What really bothers me is that there is a wonderful woman in my life who is my best friend, and I sometimes think of dating her, but I always think so sexually and degradingly about her. I can't imagine that she could ever satisfy me in the ways I see it done in porn.

See what I mean? You start using porn to excite you in ways that would have disgusted you when you started out.

Soon, things escalate *outside* the cyber realm, and you even begin using *real* women in ways that would have disgusted you in the beginning. Just as porn's escalation can stretch your sexual horizons until you can enjoy porn depicting homosexuality and sex with animals, porn can push you into bizarre, irresponsible thought patterns about sex with real girls, perhaps based upon their race or nationality. For instance, I had regular sex with a French graduate student, not because I felt any strong attraction to her, but simply because of the reputation of the French as lovers. Another time I seduced a beautiful Vietnamese woman simply because I'd never had sex with an Asian woman and wanted to see what it was like. Back at porn's starting gate, I'd have never believed it possible that I'd end up using women in such disgustingly selfish ways.

Phase 5: Desensitization

Eventually your sexual systems overload, and you become numb to it all. When you reach this stage, even the most graphic, degrading porn won't excite you anymore. You become desperate to feel the same level of thrill again, but you can't find it.

If it's difficult to relate this "desensitization" jargon to an everyday setting, allow Sam to relate how this looks in real life:

> I have been struggling with porn since my freshman year in high
> school, which was when my family got connected to the Internet.
> Once I got home from school, I'd go visit my favorite porn sites for
> an hour or so until my parents got home from work. Things escalated,
> which led to worse things, like getting involved in cybersex and even
> phone sex. I'm at the point where when I watch a movie with nudity,
> breasts do nothing for me. I guess that's the way it goes.

When desensitization worsens, some guys develop an aversion to getting personally involved with women. Their comfort zone is with women they can never meet—the porn stars found in XXX films and XXX web sites. They prefer to stay in their apartments and have sex with themselves while visiting the brothels of cyberspace. These guys have been so brainwashed by Internet porn that they're unwilling to make an effort to develop a relationship with a real live woman.

When I made this point during my talk at Iowa State, one of the student "experts" reacted sharply to this idea when he blogged, "Come on! Do any of you out there actually prefer porn and not real contact with women? I think that's just a bunch of Christian [nonsense]."

But David Amsden, a writer for the *New York Metro* magazine, would strongly disagree. In his article "Not Tonight, Honey, I'm Logging On," he wrote about Rick, who despite his good looks, had become intimidated by women. "Girls…are waiting for Derek Jeter to walk in, or a movie star, or a fifty-year-old guy to be their sugar daddy," he explains. "They want someone at the pinnacle of his career, who lives on Fifth Avenue—not someone who lives in Williamsburg with two other dudes."

Rick had a solution—of sorts. "Thing is, you can find a million girls just like them online," he says. "And they're naked, doing whatever you want them to do." Often he finds himself stumbling home after a night on the town and immediately going online to search out digital copies of the women he saw gyrating on the dance floor earlier that evening.

Amsden went on to write:

Over beers recently, a twenty-six-year-old businessman friend shocked me by casually remarking, "Dude, all of my friends are so obsessed with Internet porn that they can't sleep with their girlfriends unless they act like porn stars." A twenty-year-old college student who bartends at a popular Soho lounge describes how an I-porn-filled adolescence shaped his perceptions of sex. "Looking at Internet porn was pretty much my sex education," he says. "On the Internet, you had it all. I remember the first time I had sex, my first thought as it was happening was, *Oh, this is pornography.* It was a kind of out-of-body experience. I was really uncomfortable with sex for a while."

In many ways, a kind of "porn creep" takes over. Jacob, a Christian twenty-something, told me that after watching porn videos for a couple of years, he met a beautiful woman at work. "She was pretty provocative, and I knew she was open for anything, so I took her out of town on a three-day weekend to a nice resort. The room came with a hot tub on the balcony and a giant round bed—the works. I did everything to her I'd ever seen in my porn videos, and she did the same to me. She told me that I was 'way great,' but you know something? When it was all over, it really hit me. I hadn't felt a thing."

Jacob sought to find the same intensity he'd felt watching the videos, but he couldn't find it with a real woman anymore, even in a glorious resort hotel room, because she couldn't take him where his own hands and fantasies had taken him with porn. In short, porn and masturbation will creep in and take over your sexual makeup, eventually frying your natural inclinations to a crisp.

Phase 6: Acting Out Sexually

At this point, some guys make a dangerous jump and move from the paper, plastic, and pixel images of porn to the real world of strip clubs and prostitutes, bringing their porn viewing to life. When it came to porn, I never reached phase 5's desensitization or phase 6's acting out sexually by watching living, breathing women strip or by having sex with complete strangers, but do you suppose I had enough self-inflicted wounds to my sexuality to go around? You bet I did. In spite of all that, I didn't have a clue that I was hurting myself at the time, which is exactly what the Enemy wanted me to believe. Perhaps you've been sitting in that same boat.

Peeking Below the Surface

Once you peek below the surface at the broad damage inflicted by porn, a total cutoff of sensuality looks like a no-brainer. It's instantly clear why a mother warning her son, "I don't want you watching that trashy *The Real World* show on MTV," is no more old-fashioned than a mother warning, "Don't play on the highway." Both are risky pastimes, and you can get run over either place. It's also clear why the Father warns His sons to avoid every hint of sexual immorality. It's not because He's a grouch but because He loves you and wants to keep you normal.

The problem is, if you're like most young men today, there's already been a change in the way you see women and even in your ability to recognize sensuality itself, and this blindness is one of the reasons we don't always win quickly in this battle for purity. Your sexual senses just aren't working right. Even when you *think* you're starving the sumo, he's actually feasting big time on the side as you allow far more sensuality into your life than you should.

Bottom line, you've lost track of what normal is due to addiction's damage, and because of that, you're often working against the Lord in His efforts to restore you. To engage the battle effectively on the physical front is to find your way back to normal again. Trouble is, normal may not be too easy to find, and your desensitized eyes may hamper you as you try to track it down. I'll shed a little light on your search in the next chapter.

For Personal Reflection

1. Do you own the field yet? During a given day, what images or thoughts are still tripping you up?
2. Do you recognize any of the six phases of addiction in your own life and relationships? Give some examples.
3. Is it possible that while you think you are starving the sumo completely, he's actually still feasting far more than you know? Why

doesn't passing your thirteenth birthday automatically make PG-13 movies okay for you? If you are careful to watch only the prime-time shows your Christian friends watch, why doesn't that necessarily keep your sumo completely starved?

4

Back to the Future

I was having dinner with the family one night when Michael looked up from his plate of meatloaf and corn on the cob. "Mom, there was a girl at school who was dressed really inappropriately today in one of my classes," he said casually, picking at his food.

With an arched eyebrow, Brenda responded, "Oh?"

"Yeah, her top sunk down real low, and her back was almost totally bare. And…um…well, I don't know quite how to say this. She was sticking out a lot up top."

I laughed. *Well said!* I thought.

"Did you have any trouble bouncing your eyes like Dad has taught you?" Brenda asked.

"No," he said, "but she really made me mad that she wore that."

Michael felt that way because he's heard about the "every man's battle" stuff since he was in elementary school, and he knew that bouncing his eyes away was a normal response for a Christian guy, a reflection of discipline and character.

Are you thinking, *Michael doesn't seem very normal to me! I don't know many guys who'd respond to girls like that, so from where I stand, he looks more abnormal than normal?*

Don't confuse the concept of "common" with "normal." As you know from the last two chapters, guys who think normally about sex and girls are always going to be hard to find in this country, even within the church. But from God's point of view, Michael's reaction was exceptionally normal. You see, for a Christian, "normal" means thinking the way God thinks and then acting accordingly. God doesn't measure normal in relation to the world; He measures it in relation to the Word. Becoming normal is exactly what Christianity is all about:

> Therefore, my dear friends, as you have always obeyed—not only in my presence, but now much more in my absence—continue *to work out your salvation* with fear and trembling, for it is God who works in you to will and to act according to his good purpose.
>
> Do everything without complaining or arguing, so *that you may become blameless and pure, children of God without fault in a crooked and depraved generation, in which you shine like stars in the universe* as you hold out the word of life. (Philippians 2:12–16)

To "work out our salvation" means we are to work to become normal Christian men—blameless and pure and without fault in the midst of our lost generation, in the same way Jesus walked normally in the midst of His. When the Father spoke out about Jesus on the Mount of Transfiguration, He left no doubt that we should consider Jesus to be our perfect mark of normal:

> While [Peter] was still speaking, a bright cloud enveloped them, and a voice from the cloud said, "This is my Son, whom I love; with him I am well pleased. Listen to him!" (Matthew 17:5)

Simply put, we must listen well and become fervent and anxious to become normal, exactly as Jesus lived it out in the Word. Since we know the Bible defined "normal" for us by recording His life on earth, we also know that Jesus was the most normal guy who ever walked the face of the planet.

In short, Jesus is our standard of measure, and God uses His life (along with the rest of Scripture) to show us how normal guys handle their sexuality. Because of that, it's quite easy to pick up on the trail of the normal Christian guy in the Word, no matter how uncommon it is to find one in the world.

For instance, God says it's normal for a Christian guy to "keep his way pure" (Psalm 119:9) and to set "no vile thing" before his eyes (Psalm 101:3). God says it's normal for a guy to be *extremely* careful about what he views in prime time and at his favorite cineplex. A normal guy would *never* watch Kate Winslet stretch nude across her couch as she did in *Titanic*. He avoids lusting after girls (see Job 31:1) and hasn't "a hint of sexual immorality" in his life (Ephesians 5:3).

A normal guy doesn't hoot it up at the Hooters' girls. He isn't a voyeur, and he doesn't have "eyes full of adultery" (2 Peter 2:14). He doesn't worm his way into the homes of weak-willed young women to use them sexually (see 2 Timothy 3:6), even as their trusting parents watch FOX News in their master bedroom. Instead, he treats his sisters with absolute purity (see 1 Timothy 5:2). He guards his *own* heart by keeping his eyes straight ahead (where they belong) and by putting away perverted thoughts and conversation (see Proverbs 4:23–26). He wouldn't dream of hashing through a dicey list of "things to do before graduating" with a girl or dallying about the adult section of a video store simply because "she's always wanted to." He feels that way, not because he's terrified of God's wrath, but because he loves Him so. The Lord's grace has taught him to say no to ungodliness (see Titus 2:11–12), and it isn't normal to use grace's freedom as a cover-up for sin (see 1 Peter 2:16).

It's easy to paint a picture of normal with the Scriptures, isn't it? And gratefully, because of that, it's easy to spot how far your own sexuality has drifted off His normal line, no matter how far the porn has desensitized your eyes or how abnormal "normal" might appear to you these days. Read the last two paragraphs again, and compare your own life to the picture painted there. Have you drifted off-line? If you were never taught to guard your eyes in your early teens, you probably have.

But now take another look at Michael's reaction to that curvy girl in his classroom. Is he abnormal or normal? In light of Scripture, it's clear he's quite normal and tuned in to God's wavelength when it comes to viewing half-naked girls.

God wants to tune you back to normal too so that you can have a normal future, sexually and otherwise. But while it may be obvious why God wants you back to normal, it may *not* be so obvious how He'll manage to get you there again. How can He possibly de-escalate your sexuality and resensitize your eyes to work properly again? How can He transform you from being a voyeuristic Peeping Tom to becoming a "Keeping Tom"—a keeper of your promises to the Lord when it comes to sexual purity?

Paul has some answers for you. He spoke of such transformation in the Word:

> I appeal to you therefore, brethren, and beg of you in view of [all] the mercies of God, to make a decisive dedication of your bodies [presenting all your members and faculties] as a living sacrifice, holy (devoted, consecrated) and well pleasing to God, which is your reasonable (rational, intelligent) service and spiritual worship.
>
> Do not be conformed to this world (this age), [fashioned after and adapted to its external, superficial customs], but be transformed (changed) by the [entire] renewal of your mind [by its new ideals and its new attitude]. (Romans 12:1–2, AMP)

It's the conforming to the world—you know, calling abnormal things normal—that does us in as Christians. God wants you to stop conforming to this world's picture and to start conforming to the biblical picture instead. You do that by renewing your mind through a washing with the Word and regeneration by the Holy Spirit, by consecrating yourself, setting yourself apart, and choosing to sacrifice your will in favor of His will. This triggers the transformation back to normal.

Coincidentally, these two steps—first conforming and then transforming—more or less stake out the two war fronts in every young man's battle. *Conforming* to His Word is the tactical action you take on the physical front of the battle, through the Spirit's fruit of self-control. The *transforming* of your heart and mind is the tactical action taken on the spiritual front of the battle, through God's grace and renewal.

Conforming must be the first step. In other words, you can forget about transformation and total victory until you conform tightly to the Word.

If anyone knows that, I do. For years I asked God to transform my mind and heart related to sex, but until I began cutting off the polluting, addicting, escalating, desensitizing gunk in my life, how could He do that? How could He wash my mind clean while I was still hungrily feasting on filth? How could He make me normal? I was still rocking with the things that made me abnormal in the first place, so no matter how hard I prayed, it was two steps forward and two steps back for me.

How could it be any other way? There's a natural progression of addiction in the average, everyday guy, because that's the way God made him sexually. You might as well face it. In an oversexed culture like ours, you are built to fail. Your undisciplined eyes *will* slip into this progression, not because there's something wrong with you, but because there's *nothing* wrong with you. Your unguarded sexuality *will* degrade beneath this broad load of sensual pollution, because your sexuality was never designed to handle it.

Your sexuality was created to blossom and thrive only within a tender and glorious monogamous relationship. There are no alternatives. Expand beyond that realm, and your sexuality *will* degrade in abnormal ways. If you want to win on the spiritual front and return to normal sexuality, you have to stop the pollution on the physical front.

I *do* have some good news for you, however: if you pay the price fully and cut things back far enough, returning to normal can be pretty effortless for you. Here's what one newly normal guy said:

> I read *Every Man's Battle* in three days and then again the next week. Let me tell you, I am now one of those who is recommending this series to others. I am approaching ten weeks without porn, eight without masturbation, and five without catching myself gratifying my desires through

my eyes. In fact, I've been pleasantly surprised by some of the things I've found myself looking away from. For instance, I was invited over to a friend's house with some other couples in my church, and when I walked in, there happened to be a bikini show on TV. I saw what was on and never looked back, praise the Lord. I have grown more spiritually in the past eight weeks than I had in the previous eight years, I'm sure.

Of course, that's the rub, isn't it? How can we be sure we're cutting back far enough and paying that full price? When we pay the full price, returning to normal is natural. But because of the desensitization we talked about in the last chapter, finding "far enough" may not be so easy. Most guys have been so lax in their visual standards that they often aren't even aware they're still looking at the wrong things. They think they've cleaned up their act, but they haven't; their sexual senses aren't working normally enough to recognize that point of purity. My colleague, Shannon Ethridge, got it right in *Every Woman's Battle* when she wrote we think we are "mature enough to watch any movie or television show, read any book, listen to any music, or surf any Web sites without being affected in a negative way." But that is not true.

Most of us become desensitized to what we see or hear. I've demonstrated this through an experiment I conduct when teaching about sexuality during weekend retreats for youth groups. I once recorded two hours of prime-time television shows such as *Friends* and *Seinfeld*, then edited the tape down to a twelve-minute clip including only the sexual innuendos (anything visual or auditory related to inappropriate sexual conduct). As I show this video clip, I challenge the audience to keep count during these twelve minutes of how many sexual messages they see or hear, giving me a sign (placing their thumb on their nose) to indicate that they recognize each one.

As many times as I have conducted this experiment, I'm amazed at how the same thing happens every time. They catch maybe the first three or four innuendos, but then become so engrossed in the funny scenes that they forget to give me the sign or to keep count. At the end of the twelve minutes, I ask, "How many did you count?" The average response? Eleven or twelve. The actual number of visual or verbal innuendos? Forty-one.

This may be addiction's biggest trap of all. You know you've got to cut the sensuality way back to get your eyes resensitized and back to normal, but those damaged eyes of yours trick you into believing you've gone far enough when you actually haven't come close.

This reminds me of a trip I took to a western city to take part in a radio broadcast. Upon hearing I was in town, a large church asked me to come by to say a word to its singles ministry and answer a few questions. I like Q-and-A sessions, so I happily agreed.

When I arrived at the church, I settled down in the front row with the rest of the crowd to hear the young pastor's talk about relationships. As part of the message, he showed a clip from a then-current movie, *Something's Gotta Give,* which starred Jack Nicholson and Diane Keaton and was billed as a "grown-up love story." I was simply stunned. Throughout this rather lengthy clip, I had to look at the floor because of the sensual overtone. No one else seemed to notice.

After the pastor's message, the women split off for refreshments while the guys hustled into another room for the Q and A with me. These young guys were clearly interested in purity, and I spent more than two hours answering a myriad of questions. But not once did the sensuality of *Something's Gotta Give* come up, nor did I feel comfortable broaching this subject because I was a guest.

As I drove away that night, I was filled with sadness and unsettled by the absurdity of it all: the pastor was so desensitized himself to the sensuality in films that he never realized he was firing his guys' sexual engines on the same night he'd called me to cool them down.

If your standards don't match up with God's, you can think you're walking in perfect purity when in reality you're stumbling miserably. This will still drive a wedge into your intimacy with God, and tragically, you won't know why there's a gap.

Later, when you can't seem to get completely free of sexual sin, you'll become discouraged in the battle and wonder, *What in the world is wrong with me?* Believe me, there's nothing wrong with you. Your warped, abnormal standards are still allowing enough sensual fuel to seep in and fire your engines. That's all. You think you are completely starving the sumo, but he's snacking big time on the side.

Jim, an unmarried pastor, was trapped in this way. "I don't understand why I'm not free yet! I've made some huge moves toward purity since reading *Every Man's Battle.* I've even gotten to the point where I'm wondering if I should be watching PG-13 movies anymore," he announced.

He's off to a great start but hasn't gone far enough! Many of today's PG-13 movies and popular videos pack the same dose of sexual content as R-rated films did a decade ago. For example, in Will Ferrell's PG-13-rated *Anchorman,* the camera shows a guy getting an erection while chatting up a woman, prompting her to make a funny remark. Another guy invites a woman to "party in his pants." The film's machine-gun sexual innuendos, accompanied by flashes of skin, are typical fare in today's movies.

When it comes to films, the ratings have become so useless that I've turned instead to a single overarching rule: whatever pollutes my stream is off-limits, and I'm very careful to let the Bible tell me what pollutes. After all, if you are as desensitized to sensuality as I once was, it's critical to cast Scripture in the leading role in your entertainment decisions. If you don't, you may be polluting yourself without even realizing it.

For instance, my son Jasen told me about a couple of college friends—I'll call them Andrew and Brandon—who were struggling with lust. Brandon admitted that he was feeling quite distant from God. Knowing Jasen was living strong, Andrew asked him, "What should we do?"

Jasen knew Andrew and Brandon liked to watch "horny teen" movies, but when my son suggested that perhaps their viewing habits were stoking their sexual fires, they rolled their eyes. "Give it up, Jasen," Andrew snapped. "You're so narrow minded! We're free to watch whatever we want!"

As Jasen replayed the scene for me over the phone, I mused, *They're free? That freedom is forging the very chains that have them bound, and they aren't even aware of it.*

Stories like this are common. Since God's laws of reaping and sowing work slowly and deliberately, many young men don't always connect the dots between their sin and the results. Then a low-grade sexual fever sets in, and the distance from God grows.

Was Jasen being narrow minded with his friends? I don't think so. Of course, it may *appear* narrow to those who've been calling the abnormal "normal" for too long—like those who say it is normal to sprinkle a little sensual spice over their entertainment fare.

But the bottom line is the biblical line, and that's why it wasn't Jasen who was fighting off sexual fevers. Remember, sometimes the Christian way *is* the narrower way, and that's surely the case on this physical front of the battle for purity. That also means that there are far better questions for those guys—and you—to be answering here: What price are you willing to pay to get outside the cultural box and reverse the desensitization to sensual entertainment in your life? If you still haven't broken free from your sexual sin, are you willing to take a radical step to bring your eyes back to normal, such as going on a total media sabbatical?

In the workplace, a sabbatical is a time of refreshment, a time to lay aside the busyness and get away from the ringing telephones to pursue something deeper in your heart or the world around you. When you go on a sabbatical, you don't quit your career; you simply step away for a while.

A media sabbatical is a similar endeavor: you step away from the entertainment media for two or three months while you make a deeper connection with God. This period of media inactivity—I'm talking about first-run movies, video rentals, Xbox, Nintendo, prime-time television, cable channels like MTV—will allow you to cut away every hint of immorality and focus on actual healing and depth in God. (You'll have to do something about the Internet as well, perhaps limiting yourself to e-mail and surfing the Net when a buddy is in the room. In other words, no late-night Internet. And I'm not asking you to give up watching your favorite sports on TV, although you'll want to zap to another channel during those sexually drenched beer ads.)

A multimedia sabbatical will likely have an interesting side effect. When my friend Bill was facing a divorce he didn't want, to try to save his marriage, for three months he did nothing in the evening but pray, worship, and read Christian marriage books. But after the divorce was finalized, he happened to flip on the tube one night to relax. What he saw astounded him. "I couldn't believe all the sexual talk and how shocking the wardrobes were," he said. "I guess I didn't notice all that stuff before because I'd gotten so used to it, but I am sure sensitive to it now. I'm making a big change in the shows I watch these days."

What about you? If you still aren't winning your battle for purity, could it be that your eyes are fooling you so that you are not cutting out enough sensuality? If you are blind to it, perhaps the only way you'll learn the truth is to take a couple of months off from all the shows and movies and computer games you usually watch and play. Then, once you "reboot" your systems, you should notice a difference and have a better idea about what you need to do to own the field on this physical front of the battle.

Only then will your eyes be able to tell the holy from the unholy:

You shall make a distinction and recognize a difference between the holy and the common or unholy, and between the unclean and the clean. (Leviticus 10:10, AMP)

Dropping the desensitized scales of blindness from your eyes could be the key that opens the door to victory in your battle for purity.

For Personal Reflection

1. What do you think is the difference between common and normal?
2. What does it mean to work out our salvation?
3. What two steps will trigger your transformation back to normal?
4. True or false: Slipping into the progression of addiction proves there is something wrong with you. Why or why not?
5. Are you willing to take a three-month media sabbatical to find out just how much your eyes have been desensitized?

A Second Kind of Blindness

Let's get right to the point. It may not be the physical "blindness" caused by the desensitization to your physical eyes that's keeping you from finding your way back to normal. Another kind of blindness may be at the root. Your barrier to victory may actually be the desensitization of your *spiritual* eyes, caused by pride or ignorance of the Word.

There is a key difference between these two kinds of blindness. Your desensitized *physical* eyes make it harder for you to *find* the boundaries that you need for the physical front of the battle. But desensitized *spiritual* eyes make it tough to recognize that *any* lines need to be drawn at all! In fact, it gets so tough that some men actually view this spiritual desensitization as a good thing—as just that healthy maturation of "liberty" and "grace" in the heart that every good, solid believer needs. Nothing could be further from the truth. Brian wrote this:

> I noticed in the *Every Single Man's Battle Workbook* where you said that
> you only watch family-friendly films. I was curious if you could go into
> a little more detail for me? Every Christian man I know says he can
> watch anything he wants, and he justifies this by saying that God
> knows his heart. My friends attack me because I find fault in almost

everything currently on television or movies. I desperately want direction and guidance in my life on this.

"God knows his heart"? What a puzzling defense of sinful behavior! It's absolutely true that God knows what's in our hearts, but that shouldn't be too comforting, given what the Bible tells us He knows. For instance, He knew that our hearts would argue when we were told to avoid every hint of sexual immorality (see Ephesians 5:3), so He warned us three verses later (see verses 6–7) that He absolutely meant what He had just said, admonishing us not to allow our hearts to be fooled by empty arguments to the contrary.

He knows that our hearts are deceitful and easily fooled (see Jeremiah 17:9). In fact, we're so easily fooled that many "Christians" will one day swear on a stack of Bibles that they had once given their hearts to Jesus, when they had never actually done so at all (see Matthew 7:21–23).

Because the Bible tells us what God knows about our hearts in general, we should be able to figure out how God feels about the "God knows my heart" defense without too much trouble. But in this case, we don't even have to do the figuring. This moldy-oldie idea hit the airwaves so long ago that it made it into the pages of the Bible itself. We don't have to guess what God thinks about this argument. He always takes an extremely dim view of those who use His grace as their excuse for sin:

They are godless men, who change the grace of our God into a license
for immorality. (Jude 1:4)

This position that "God knows my heart and so He isn't concerned about what I watch" just doesn't make sense biblically. Yes, I'm aware that the Bible allows some leeway for personal convictions to guide our lives in areas the Word doesn't address clearly. But sexuality is not one of those areas.

Paul wrote plainly in his letter to the Ephesians that we must avoid every hint of sexual immorality (see Ephesians 5:3) and not even joke about these things (see verse 4). In fact, we aren't to even mention what the lost are doing sexually in private (see verse 12). Now, if it's not right to even *speak* about these things when we come together, how can it be right to *watch* them depicted when we gather in front of DVD players or in theaters? How could Paul have been any more clear?

Yet Christ Himself was even *clearer* when He sent His *own* direct message to the Ephesians. Brian's friends would do well to note what the Lord thinks of their logic:

> Yet I hold this against you: You have forsaken your first love. Re-
> member the height from which you have fallen! Repent and do
> the things you did at first. If you do not repent, I will come to you
> and remove your lampstand from its place. *But you have this in your*
> *favor: You hate the practices of the Nicolaitans, which I also hate.* (Reve-
> lation 2:4–6)

The Nicolaitans believed spiritual liberty gave them leeway to practice sexual immorality, but Jesus *praised* the Ephesians for hating that. Today, too many guys believe that their spiritual liberty gives them the leeway to watch any sensual slop they want. Can Jesus possibly praise them for that? No way! He hates the whole idea.

The Nicolaitans probably believed that they were good, solid, mature believers—just like the guys using the "God knows my heart" argument today. But as we've seen, Jude, Paul, and Jesus would never agree with that assessment, and neither would the apostle John, for that matter. He cautioned that if anyone loves the world—the cravings of sinful man, the lust of his eyes— the love of the Father is not in him (see 1 John 2:15–16).

So exactly what does it mean when a guy firmly asserts, "I'm used to watching movies like this, and I'm going to keep doing it"? Either he isn't saved, or he's incredibly deceived.

I don't know about you, but saying such a thing would be downright scary to me, not only because we've seen that our eyes can be desensitized by watching the stuff, but also because we've already seen that it is very easy to be deceived spiritually as a Christian. The Bible *also* warns that our consciences can be seared:

> The Spirit clearly says that in later times some will abandon the faith and follow deceiving spirits and things taught by demons. Such teachings come through hypocritical liars, whose consciences have been seared as with a hot iron. (1 Timothy 4:1–2)

In his e-mail, Brian said his friends attack him for being abnormal in all his faultfinding regarding the media, but he is the normal one. The truth is, if you *aren't* finding fault in almost everything currently on television or in movies, that's a huge red flag signaling that your eyes and your heart are desensitized and seared to the sensuality around you.

If true, that would be scary enough for you, but from a tactical standpoint in this war, it gets even scarier if you've been using the "God knows my heart" argument as a defense. That would prove you're so blind that you don't even know which part of the battlefield you are standing on. After all, you're using a *spiritual* defense—God knows my heart, and He's full of grace—on the *physical* front of the battlefield. How can you expect to fight effectively while doing something dangerous like that? There may be no bigger mistake you can make than to fight on the physical front as if you're standing on a spiritual front, using spiritual philosophies that simply don't apply to that realm.

You see, each battlefront is distinct, and God has made it clear in His Word that our tactics should be different on each one. Think about it for a moment. How could the "God knows my heart" defense have any impact on the physical front of this battle? Your heart's not the issue on the physical front! Your *eyes* are the issue here, and the only pertinent question to ask is whether your eyes are as disciplined as they need to be. Troy's weren't, as you'll read here:

> Before I was saved, I had some physical-only relationships with a couple of girls to satisfy my urges. After I became a Christian, I severed my ties with those girls because they stood in the way of my relationship with

Christ. I still fell short, however, when it came to those things considered "normal" for kids my age: the pornography in movies and the rampant sexuality on television. Every time I watched a sensuous movie, I would pray the same thing over and over again: *God, I'm sorry that I'm weak and continue to fail You. If You just give me the strength to overcome the temptations, I can beat this cycle.* I still felt powerless, though, and before long, I was back in the same place I started, no farther down the road of breaking this vise grip of my sexuality.

Why did Troy still feel powerless after prayer? Because he was still abusing his "drug." Look, if you were hooked on heroin, your battle would be clearly physical, right? Working a syringe into a vein would make you as high as a kite, prompting your brain's pleasure centers to demand another hit right away. You'd never expect to get free by saying, "I can shoot up with any kind of heroin anytime I want. God understands my heart."

How ridiculous! If you thought this way, you'd be fighting a *physical* battle with a kind of *spiritual* philosophy—and a warped one, to boot. Even if God *did* understand your heart and motives behind your viewing habits in the way that you claim, it still couldn't carry you to victory on the physical front of the battle. As long as you keep mainlining visual sensuality through your eyes, you'll stay hooked. That's just the way it is, because that's the way your eyes are made.

That's why there's something different about this sin, and many of us have learned this the hard way. Remember what Terry said in the last chapter?

When I became a Christian, I quit fooling around sexually with girls. I quit cold turkey. I stopped drugs, quit swearing, and stopped smoking and drinking. I turned my life around, to Him be the honor and the glory. The only thing I couldn't kick was the porn.

When it came to battling addictions, Terry found that porn addictions are in a league of their own. The apostle Paul said the same thing:

Flee from sexual immorality. All other sins a man commits are out-side his body, but he who sins sexually sins against his own body.
(1 Corinthians 6:18)

We often think of drunkenness as a sin against the body, but not Paul. He pointedly left alcohol out of the "sins against the body" club, and I'm quite sure Terry would agree with his assessment.

Of course alcohol abuse and sexual sins are both "against the body" in one sense, because of the highs and the addictions they can both cause in the brain. But in another real sense, they stand worlds apart. After all, with alcohol it is a simple matter to remove the "means to sin"; you can simply walk away from a beer or toss it in the trash.

Not so with sexual sin, because the "means to sin" is right inside you. You can't walk away from your eyes and their ability to perform foreplay. If you want to get your mind racing, sexual images are always just a look away. That's why this sexual sin is in its own special category and why Paul gives us a unique prescription for handling it: you've got to flee.

This tactic is critical because your spiritual strength is not designed to trump sexual sewage. It's a cause-and-effect matter. If you dump sewage into your stream, it will become polluted. If your eyes aren't fleeing, you're going down. It's just that simple, as Casey attests:

Ever since I've been committed to Christ, I've never had a problem with sexual immorality. Even in my "BC" days, I always respected women, even though my friends got a big kick out of porn and slandering girls.

Basically what happened is this. Throughout my entire Christian walk, I always realized that I wasn't strong enough to watch *American Pie* or anything remotely like that. I saw the danger in it and always stayed away, and so I stayed very pure and never struggled like the other guys I knew.

Well, when I became a Fellowship of Christian Athletes leader and heavily involved with the youth group at my church, I began to think that I could start watching those kinds of movies because I was somehow "strong enough" spiritually to handle that stuff. Maybe that was the devil talking...or my pride.

Late one night I was channel surfing when I came upon a soft-core film on one of the cable channels. Like I said, I really thought I could handle it, but before long, I was handling something else. Before I knew it, I was masturbating again. I was like, *Wow, I forgot how awesome this felt.*

That evening opened up the floodgates, and I soon got into porn again and back into the sexual sins that Christ had conquered in my life a long time ago. Instead of being man enough to take care of it every time I messed up, I would say to myself, *This is the last time, really. I'm fine. I'm a strong Christian. God knows my heart.* So I wouldn't bring it up at my accountability meetings or anything.

Notice the foolish mistake Casey made here. His spiritual strength *was* very admirable, but it was still impotent to protect him on the physical front of the battle because it's not really a heart issue here. It's an eye issue. He wasn't immune because of his strong spirituality; none of us are. When he began sinning against his body, he reaped what he sowed, just as God said he would. It is "discipline or die" on this front of the battle, no matter how high you're waving God's flag of grace.

God will not be mocked. He didn't tell you to flee sexual immorality until you were spiritually strong enough to stand it. He told you to flee...period. It's the fleeing—bouncing the eyes, starving the sumo—that keeps your body from being captured on the physical front of the battle. These are the proper weapons here.

That's why your victory on the physical front doesn't depend upon how much God loves you or how much He understands your heart. Here, it only matters how much you are obeying. How far have your eyes been desensitized by the years of addiction? How much food have you been feeding your sumo sex drive without realizing it? The answers to these key questions will determine the outcome.

His Spiritual Role

Now, that's not to say that God has no role on the physical front of the battlefield. He does, and He fulfilled His role at Calvary and continues playing His role today through the Holy Spirit by relentlessly fanning your desire for purity.

Besides that, the new life of Christ is in you, so your practical effort to put up defenses on the physical front never happens without His spiritual power. It is always a spiritual effort when you choose to walk in alignment with the Spirit, because that new life of Christ is in you. You two are inseparable. As we said earlier, God has provided everything you need to obey Him on this front:

> ...seeing that His divine power has granted to us everything pertaining to life and godliness, through the true knowledge of Him who called us by His own glory and excellence. For by these He has granted to us His precious and magnificent promises, so that by them you may become partakers of the divine nature, having escaped the corruption that is in the world by lust. (2 Peter 1:3–4, NASB)

But *your* role here is also clear, and watching anything you want doesn't meet your responsibility in this role. On this physical front, your call is to conform to the Word, and according to what God says, *your* choices and efforts are absolutely critical.

- You're responsible to *offer* all the parts of your body—including your eyes and your genitals—as instruments of righteousness (see Romans 6:11–14).

- You are to *choose* to live a "holy and godly" life and to "make every *effort* to be found spotless, blameless and at peace with him" (see 2 Peter 3:11–14).

- As a slave to righteousness (see Romans 6:16–18), you must *choose* to purify yourself from everything that contaminates your body and spirit, perfecting your holiness out of your reverence for God (see 2 Corinthians 7:1).

- You must never conform to this world (see Romans 12:1–2) but rather *choose* to avoid all sexual immorality (see 1 Thessalonians 4:3–8), *choose* to put aside all deeds of darkness (see Romans 13:11–12), and *choose* to crucify your sinful nature, including all of its passions and desires, to keep in step with the Spirit's call (see Galatians 5:16–25).

You will never get back to normal in the way you view women until you follow the Word by making these choices on the physical front. But once you do make them, both the desensitization of your eyes and your spiritual blindness will begin to fade, and normal won't be as hard to find.

For Personal Reflection

1. What causes the desensitization of your spiritual eyes?
2. When it comes to drawing lines in the battle for purity, what is the key difference between having desensitized physical eyes and having desensitized spiritual eyes?
3. Even if God understands your heart, why isn't that enough to make you victorious on the physical front of the battle?
4. Why do you think the apostle Paul placed sexual sin in a category of its own?
5. Why won't our spiritual strength guarantee us victory in the battle?

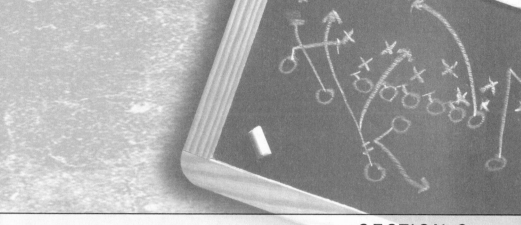

THE SPIRITUAL FRONT OF THE BATTLE

Searching for Intimacy

"Teacher, which is the greatest commandment in the Law?"
Jesus replied: " 'Love the Lord your God with all your heart
and with all your soul and with all your mind.'
This is the first and greatest commandment.
And the second is like it: 'Love your neighbor as yourself.'
All the Law and the Prophets hang on
these two commandments."

MATTHEW 22:36–40

Your victory on the spiritual front of the battle hangs on these two commandments too. If you obey them, you will grow a deep, genuine intimacy
with God and with your brothers in Christ. That's good, because finding intimacy with God and your neighbor is your prime objective on the spiritual

front. Intimacy transforms your old mind into the mind of Christ and keeps you connected with those around you. Intimacy changes every young man's battle forever.

Of course, you still have to get there, don't you? It's rarely easy, because whenever you make a move toward God, there will always be collateral damage in your life and in your relationships. This damage carries a lot of confusion with it, sometimes souring your attitudes toward God and increasing the disconnection you feel toward the people around you. You certainly can't afford that on this battlefield, since disconnection always works in the Enemy's favor here.

Over the next four chapters we'll take a look at how a lack of intimacy with God and with your neighbors can affect your fight for purity.

But before we do, please read these words once more: finding intimacy with God and your neighbor is your prime objective on the spiritual front. Intimacy transforms your old mind into the mind of Christ and keeps you connected with those around you. Intimacy changes every young man's battle forever.

If you don't pause here to understand that genuine connection is your chief goal on this other front, you may have trouble tracking with me as I lay out how emotional wounds affect your sexuality and how division between you and your friends can take your purity down the tubes.

This battlefront is quite distinct from the other one. On the physical front, you fight to get your eyes and mind in order. On the spiritual front, you fight to get your heart in order. It's not so much about what you *do* over here but how you *connect.*

In short, you are turning a sharp corner as you turn this page, stepping directly from one battlefront to the other. Soon you'll learn how God's grace teaches your heart to say no to ungodliness and yes to real connection with your teammates in Christ.

6

Collateral Damage

After the Marshalltown game, Michael peeled off his helmet and shoulder pads and skipped past the team bus, climbing instead into our car for the sixty-minute ride home. He knew his teammates weren't stopping to eat on the way, and after hand fighting that gorilla all night long, he was starved.

Spotting a pair of golden arches on the horizon, I pulled in and ordered the usual for him: a number-two Extra Value Meal with a Coke. He thanked me, inhaled the two cheeseburgers in about six bites, wolfed down the fries, and then kicked back with a restful sigh, musing pensively as the darkened fields of corn and soybeans raced by.

"Do you wish you were back on the bus with the team?" I ventured.

"Not really. I enjoyed the ride over to the game, though. It's great to get a quiet break like that before a game," he said.

"Quiet? I thought things would be pretty rowdy on the bus ride," I remarked.

"I suppose so," he said, "but I don't fit in that well."

His seemingly casual comment sacked me for a big loss. Michael is quite outgoing at school and extremely funny, keeping us in stitches at home with all of his little quirks, smirks, and commentary.

"What exactly do you mean, Son?" I inquired.

"Well, the guys in the locker room asked me last week why I'm not going out with anyone at school," he said.

"So, what'd ya say?"

"I told them I'm only thirteen and don't think I'm old enough to be dating."

I chuckled uneasily. The picture was coming into focus.

"They also found out that I mostly watch G-rated movies, and they laughed at me out loud," he said with a chuckle of his own. "They think I'm weird."

The car became quiet as he directed his eyes back to the cornfields. As for me, my mind turned back to my playing days at Thomas Jefferson High, a blue-collar school built on the west side of Cedar Rapids among rail yards, meat-packing plants, grain processors, and ramshackle half-a-century-old homes. Where I came from, nobody laughed at a guy tough enough to start both ways on the line of scrimmage. Well, okay, I take that back. Sometimes we laughed at Mack because he was so musclebound he couldn't scratch his own back, but we laughed then because we were jealous of him.

Still, given my past, Michael's comment blew me away. When I broke the silence, my first reaction was predictable.

"What a bunch of coneheads! You're a two-way starter! Who cares what you do off the field?"

"Don't get me wrong, Dad. They respect me and everything. I just don't always get included in the celebrations and the laughter like the other starters."

Another quiet pause. And I suppose my second reaction came out much better. "You know, Son, now that I think about it, neither of us should be surprised by this. Your teammates' reactions were prophesied about two thousand years ago."

Intrigued, Michael turned and asked, "What do you mean, Dad?"

"Well, Peter wrote about this in one of his letters in the Bible. I've got it memorized: 'For you have spent enough time in the past doing what pagans choose to do—living in debauchery, lust, drunkenness, orgies, carousing and detestable idolatry. They think it strange that you do not plunge with them into the same flood of dissipation, and they heap abuse on you. But they will have to give account to him who is ready to judge the living and the dead.' That's from 1 Peter 4:3–5. Michael, they think you're strange for a similar reason, don't they?"

"They sure do," he said, nodding. "In fact, do you remember those guys who leave practice early on Wednesday nights so they can make it to youth group on time? Even they think I'm strange."

"You're strange?" My thoughts heated up again: *Michael is talking about a bunch of guys who leave football practice early to go to youth group, but their lifestyles are exactly the same as non-Christians, which means they don't look the least bit odd to the rest of their teammates. And then they have the audacity to call my son strange. How bizarre is that?*

I pulled myself together and asked, "Remember how God says we are to shine like stars in this crooked universe of ours?"

"Yes, I remember that," Michael answered.

"Well, stars look an awful lot different from darkness, don't they? You'll never shine like a star without looking a lot different from everyone else. So don't worry that something is wrong with you. There isn't anything wrong with you. In fact, this just means that something is right with you, according to the apostle Peter. If people weren't making a little fun of you, that would be the time to start worrying. It's been that way for two thousand years, and that's how it's always going to be."

My son nodded his understanding.

"Michael, this probably sounds crazy, but being laughed at by your teammates is something to be proud of," I continued. "It means you're becoming a man and aren't afraid to stand up and be who you say you are. Some guys never get to that place no matter how long they live."

You're One of His

It's normal for Christians to look different and to be misunderstood. God told us ahead of time it would be this way for His children, and that news should be freeing to you. After all, it's encouraging proof that you're one of His and doing just fine by Him. He wants you to rejoice when classmates heap abuse on you:

> Blessed are you when men hate you,
>> when they exclude you and insult you
>> and reject your name as evil,
>>> because of the Son of Man.
>
> Rejoice in that day and leap for joy, because great is your reward in heaven. (Luke 6:22–23)

I know this can be tough to get your head around, because it's certainly no picnic when friends or acquaintances pile on at school. And it can be downright disorienting when it's your own brothers and sisters in Christ diving onto the dog pile. I made this same point in *Every Young Man's Battle* when I told a story about Cyndi, a high-school student with high standards who loved living radically for God.

I asked her one time if it was hard to hold on to her high standards.

"Oh, I don't mind being mocked," she replied. "Christ was mocked plenty. That's just part of it."

The sincerity of her statement blew me away. I was about to say something when I noticed a large tear roll down her right cheek.

"What's wrong?" I inquired.

"I so ache to find a friend, anyone, who's like me," she whispered.

My heart practically broke for her, and I wondered how her friends could be so mushy about their standards. And why were young women like Cyndi, who *had* standards, so lonely?

I heard from a bunch of readers who told me that Cyndi's story touched them as well, but I guarantee you, not one reader came close to being touched as deeply as I was by that huge tear and crumpled face. You see, "Cyndi" was my daughter Laura. I used a pseudonym in *Every Young Man's Battle,* because she was still in high school. But now that she's a young adult in college and I have her permission, I can share the rest of her story.

Shortly after that conversation with my daughter, Laura's youth pastor, Larry, moved on. Pastor Larry had preached a pretty straight biblical line, and while he was there, Laura managed to cobble together a handful of young people to run with.

Sadly, after Larry left, the biblical lines began to fade in the youth group. Little was done to promote godly standards, and seldom were the lessons based upon Scripture. The results were predictable: right and wrong became quite blurred.

For instance, one Wednesday night the group was asked to pay attention to a little promotion for an upcoming spiritual retreat weekend, which would feature a disco dance on Saturday night. The lights were turned down, and three girls bounced out in tight, low-cut black dresses and began dancing and thrusting to a strong disco beat. My daughters were stunned by the heavy sensuality.

When they told me what had happened, I inquired, "What exactly were they doing?"

"I can't name the dance, but it was plenty vulgar," Laura replied.

"You can say that again," Rebecca said with disgust.

They said the guys were clapping, whistling, hooting, and begging for more. As they spoke, I pondered if the evening's theme was "Wounding Your Purity Night"?

One night as the gang talked about where to hang out for the evening, Laura offered our place. That idea was immediately batted down by Mark, the most popular guy in her circle. Mark had told me once how much he loved the message of *Every Young Man's Battle,* but after months of hearing soft, weak teaching, his respect for that message had clearly grown cold.

"Let's not go to Laura's," he announced rudely. "We can never watch anything cool on television over there, and it's boring." His friends laughed and loudly agreed.

Laura died inside. When she got back home, she sat and cried for a very long time. As I held her, I thought back to that conversation we'd had a year or two earlier when she had sniffled, "I so ache to find a friend, anyone, who's like me." *She's already hurting so much, and now this!* I thought. Sadder still, neither of us had seen anything yet. This pattern repeated itself over the next two years.

Laura was far too strong, too pretty, and too talented to quit, of course. She still dreamed of being a veterinarian, an aspiration she'd nurtured since she was three years old. She still had her close-knit family, and best of all she still had Jesus. So, as her youth group dissolved around her, she moved on to Plan B and threw her whole heart into her schoolwork and, later, college, where she has a new set of awesome friends and roommates.

Still, I'll never forget an indelible moment during our last "date" the night before she moved onto campus. All day long we had been packing and racing to stores to purchase last-minute necessities for her dorm room. When we were done, the family van was filled to the corners.

We slipped over to Starbucks, where she ordered a hot chocolate and I asked for a grande coffee and cream. Soon our quiet conversation shifted to old memories of life and living. We devoted a wonderful hour to kicking through old times and sharing how much we loved each other. Finally the time came to head back for her last night in her old bed. I couldn't resist asking her one last question. "Laura, what is the very best thing about going off to college, the one thing that you'll appreciate most about heading out to your new life?"

Her smile faded quickly. She turned slightly and painfully stared across the highway and into the night. Once again I saw her face crumple. "That I'll never be hurt by that youth group again!" she blurted. Then Laura fell into my arms in wrenching sobs.

My own tears pooled as her shoulders shook. Several moments passed before Hebrews 10:32–33 bubbled up into my consciousness: "Remember those earlier days…when you stood your ground in a great contest in the face of suffering. Sometimes you were publicly exposed to insult and persecution; at other times, you stood side by side with those who were so treated."

A bitter thought crowded my consciousness. *And sometimes you are publicly insulted and persecuted by the very ones who are standing with you!* I was angry at Christianity at that moment, and while I knew that Hebrews 10:32–33 was supposed to be encouraging, that night God's Word fell miles short for me. So did the verse that urges a guy to rejoice when the people around you hate you, exclude you, and insult you.

Expect to Be Dumped On by Christians Too

Over time (and after some pretty direct revelation from the Lord, which I'll discuss later), my anger faded as I realized that this brother-dumping-on-brother stuff had *also* been prophesied from the beginning. You can always expect the world to dump on you, but in messy cultural times like these, you can expect stones and arrows from other Christians as well:

> Because of the increase of wickedness, the love of most will grow cold. (Matthew 24:12)

Matthew could have been writing about today's America. Let's face it, wickedness *is* increasing at unprecedented rates, at least in terms of pornography and sexual sin. And these increases have spawned countless cold hearts toward God, even within the church. It's no secret that Christians in this country have a bad habit of identifying themselves as Christians and then doing whatever they want. Had you asked me early on what surprised me most about Christianity after my salvation, I would have answered how few Christians actually cared whether their lives matched up to Christ's.

Given what Matthew wrote, I'm no longer surprised, but it still bothers me because it multiplies the price young people must pay when they step out to walk purely before God. The confusion, frustration, and indignation you feel makes it that much tougher to stick to your standards when your own brothers and sisters are mocking you. And it can get awfully hard to tell who's right and who's wrong spiritually amid the laughter and loneliness that follow.

It's gotten so bad that it's become useless to measure the health of a youth group or campus ministry by its size or its facilities—or even by its entertainment value. Far more useful measures would be the answers to these questions:

- Can a guy take a strong step toward living like Christ and not get hammered for it?
- Will he still be included as part of the gang, or will he have to look outside the group for friends?
- Can he maintain the courage of his own convictions if he continues to mix with the Christians around him?

Ben is hanging on by a thread:

I just read *Every Young Man's Battle,* and I would like to write to thank you for writing such a great book. It has reaffirmed my faith in Christ and shown me that I'm not the only young man trying to remain sexually pure, and that means the world to me right now, especially in light of the relationship I began with Michelle three months ago.

At first, everything was fine, but as the relationship went on, I began hanging out with her friends. Over time, they'd drop names of the different guys she'd gone out with before me. From what I can tell, she didn't have sex with them, but it sounds like she made out with just about everybody. I've counted eighteen different guys she's gone out with, including the five she met while studying overseas last semester. She even allowed a couple of those to take off her shirt and bra!

Her friends claim that this shouldn't be a big deal to me because the past is the past, and that really bothers me. How can they say that? I mean, these guys got to second base with my girlfriend, and she barely knew them! They were strangers, just hooking up for the entertainment.

I've been very rattled by this, and it's caused me to stumble in many ways. First, I've lost a lot of respect for her and for young Christian women in general. Second, I've fallen back into pornography, a habit I had beaten earlier when I was hanging around some strong Christian guys. I don't want to continue backsliding into the porn because it only makes my situation worse—it makes it too easy to think about her with those other guys.

I desperately want to shut off my imagination! It feels like they have a part of her that I can't have, and now that she's had her fun and wants to settle down, my only honor is to be the poor schmuck who gets the leftovers. We've argued over this for a couple of weeks, but I stopped bringing it up after I saw how our discussions hurt her.

But what about *my* hurt? I now find it harder and harder not to lust after women, especially her. I'm jealous that I can't live the kind of lifestyle that those other guys live, taking advantage of women and allowing myself some sexual pleasure before marriage. Why should I be a man of integrity? Having a bunch of sex doesn't appear to make a guy any less attractive to Christian women anyway.

I'm losing sight of God and finding it harder to remain monogamous and pure. Does God require that I date only one person at a time, or is it okay to date multiple girls at the same time to find a wife? Now that I feel like I'll never meet a girl of real integrity anyway, my anxiety over this has become a consuming force in my life.

Sometimes I feel too judgmental toward Michelle, because I know God still loves her and forgives her, but at the same time, she was a *Christian* when she went abroad, and yet she *still* hooked up with *five* guys. She's tried to console me by saying, "Ben, most of these guys were just friends of mine. It was nothing. We just happened to find ourselves alone together, and, well, you know, things just happen!" But things *don't* just happen. You choose what happens in life, and just because a guy is your friend doesn't make it okay to let him grab your breasts and make out.

The most confusing thing of all is that all her friends in her campus ministry act this same way. I feel like the whole Christian world is against me except for a small, select group. Most of *my* Christian friends aren't living the ideal lifestyle either, and that compounds everything.

I just can't deal with all the un-Christlike Christians around me anymore. My defenses are getting weak, and I'm afraid that I'll use Michelle sexually in the near future. No one close to me wants to walk in integrity: they keep the parts of the Bible they like and toss out the parts they don't. They say things like, "God didn't specifically say anything about that, so it must be all right to do it."

I'm tired of the burdens and the anxiety, tired of the late nights mulling this over and over and over in my head. I fear for my soul and for the souls of those around me. I fear for my relationship with Michelle, because I very much want her to be better off for having known me (as you said in *Every Young Man's Battle*), but I'm afraid that with my resolve crumbling, I'll end up grabbing her chest like everyone else.

I fear for my relationship with God, because with all the Christians around me ignoring Him and doing whatever they want, it is getting harder and harder for me to believe in Him.

Ben's angry. He's confused and discouraged, and though he's surrounded himself with Christians, he feels disconnected from nearly all of them. Anger and bitterness are always dangerous to our walk with God, because they disconnect us from others and cut us off from His river of peace.

But at least Ben has come to the realization that this anger and discouragement are dangerous in his battle for purity, even though he's not exactly sure why. Perhaps you've seen the same pattern in your life, and you're having trouble putting two and two together as well.

Even if you haven't seen this pattern in yourself, I'm sure you recognize that we're living in spiritually confusing times. But be encouraged. That's one more reason your Father is willing to stand by you and embrace your defeats with you, even as you take two steps forward and one step back. God knows how this kind of interpersonal drama in the body of Christ plays havoc with another vulnerability in your sexuality as a man—one I didn't discuss in *Every Young Man's Battle*. God wants to teach you to stand strong in the face of this second vulnerability, just as He wants to teach you how to defend your eyes. It's time to take a hard look at the role this second sexual vulnerability plays in our battle for purity.

For Personal Reflection

1. When your classmates are laughing at how different you are, what does that prove about your manhood?

2. Look in the mirror. Do you really care whether your life matches up to Christ's? List the evidence.

3. Have you gone far enough into purity that you're paying a heavy price even with your Christian friends?

4. Ponder these questions again from page 80: In your youth group or campus ministry, can a guy take a strong step toward living like Christ and not get hammered for it? Will he still be included as part of the gang, or will he have to look outside the group for friends? Can he maintain the courage of his own convictions if he continues to mix with the Christians around him?

A Second Sexual Vulnerability

I was recently horrified to hear a youth pastor stand up before his young flock
and say, "Gang, you can watch anything you like as long as you don't feel
bad about it yourself. If you don't feel bad about it in your heart, God must
be okay with it in your life." We already know this is an abomination against
the Scriptures, because we know that our eyes and our conscience can be too
seared to be trustworthy. We also know the kinds of binding cords such an
undisciplined life will wrap around us on the physical front of the battle.

But consider the further chaos it causes on the spiritual front of our battle for purity by taking this pop quiz. Which of the following two scriptures
applies the most to what this youth pastor said?

> But among you there must not be even a hint of sexual immorality, or
> of any kind of impurity. (Ephesians 5:3)

or

> In those days there was no king in Israel; every man did what was right
> in his own eyes. (Judges 21:25, AMP)

The second one, of course. The mind-set taught by this pastor creates the same kind of division in the body of Christ that it created among the tribes of Israel in the Old Testament.

Look, I understand what he was probably thinking. He wanted his guys to focus on experiencing God in His personality and power, not just in His rules. We should all want to splash about freely in His streams of liberty and grace. I vividly remember those days of aching and burning with agonizing tears for that same experience, and perhaps you yearn for it more desperately than I did. God yearns for that very same thing with you, and finding that is your first destiny and call:

> "Teacher, which is the greatest commandment in the Law?"
> Jesus replied: " 'Love the Lord your God with all your heart and with all your soul and with all your mind.' This is the first and greatest commandment." (Matthew 22:36–37)

Still, don't miss the extreme danger that's right before you. While God definitely wants you to experience the fullness of His personality, He also wants you to make sure you are seeking *His* face, not the face *you've* given Him to wear, created out of your own imagination. The key question is this: are you loving *Him* with all your heart, or are you loving that newer, more comfortable *image* of Him that you've conjured up? If you use your expectations and feelings to define God, you can't experience God in His fullness because you aren't relating to *Him* any longer; you're relating to some imaginative picture you've drawn of Him. You've created God in your own image. That's idolatry.

Creating God in your own image will severely affect your relationship with God, but it will also hurt your relationships with your brothers, as we've just seen in the last chapter. It's very divisive to the body of Christ, and the reason behind that is clear: if we're each following the Lord according to our own whims, we are no longer following *one* God but hundreds of gods, each created according to our personal images.

That kind of division is devastating to us within the context of our battle for sexual purity, and it explains why God can't and won't just let the issue of our viewing habits slide in our lives. He used Jude to warn us about this kind of division many centuries ago:

> [The apostles] said to you, "In the last times there will be scoffers who will follow their own ungodly desires." *These are the men who divide you,* who follow mere natural instincts and do not have the Spirit. (Jude 18–19)

Division—that's why God insists we all get it right on the spiritual front of the battle. It's time to take a closer look at this truth and to understand why division not only impacts our own sexual purity but also the purity of our brothers and sisters in Christ. In other words, it's time to interject some straight talk about the connection between masturbation and a guy's feelings of division, discouragement, and anger in his relationships.

I mentioned earlier that masturbation is often more an emotional issue than a sexual one, remember? This is because of a second major vulnerability in your sexual makeup.

You're already well versed about our first vulnerability, which is our ability to draw vivid sexual gratification from sensual things around us. You know very well why Satan wants you disconnected from God's *ways* on this matter: once you're far out to sea, your mutinous eyes and mind play right into his hands, working against you and your purity rather than for you.

But why would the Enemy want you disconnected from God's *people*? Because he knows this second vulnerability works like the first one. If he can keep you disconnected from others, this second weakness plays naturally into his hands and stabs a hole in your sexual defenses. In fact, this second form of disconnection is nearly as dangerous to your sexual purity as your roving eyes.

If we use these two sexual vulnerabilities as our reference points, we can distill our battle for purity down to a couple of sentences. Defending your first sexual vulnerability—your eyes and mind—is your main assignment on the *physical* front of the battle. Defending your *second* vulnerability—your rela-tionships with God and the guys around you—is your assignment on the *spir-itual* front of the battle.

But just what does this second vulnerability look like? In one sense, it looks a lot like our first one in that it simply arrives as part of the male sexual package. In other words, it's another inborn bent. By nature, men get their intimacy tanks filled from what they do prior to and during sexual intercourse. Essentially, sex is our native language of intimacy when it comes to our rela-tionships with women, and it's the language we long to use when we share inti-macy and communicate it.

Women have a different native language, and this language more naturally fills their needs for intimacy with talking, sharing, hugging, and touching. Dealing with two different languages can create all kinds of confusion for you on the relational side of things. For one, you aren't even allowed to *use* your native language outside a marital relationship, according to your Lord. That's a tall order, and it's hard to hold back from communicating this way when you fall in love. That's why guys sometimes push hard against the sexual bounda-ries of their girlfriends. It's not always because they're "godless pigs" (as my friend Lisa so eloquently puts it) but because they simply long to express their hearts in their innate language of love. Obviously, things can slide downhill quickly in your relationships if you aren't aware of this sexual bent.

But the confusion gets dramatically more serious on the physiological side of things. As I said earlier, nearly all of the body's most powerful chemicals are involved in a wash of pleasure that floods the brain's limbic centers during orgasm. That's why masturbation is such a hard habit to kick, remember?

And the fact that your natural language for communicating intimacy with women ultimately includes orgasm complicates things even further. You see, it can get confusing inside you; an orgasm from masturbation can feel a lot like intimacy to you. In other words, the pleasure chemicals released in the body during masturbation can easily become a seductively powerful substitute for that real experience of orgasm with a real woman, and it's easy to see how this happens.

First of all, an orgasm produces a strong sense of manhood in a guy. He feels dominant and strong at the moment of release, even though the sensation is fleeting. Second, he also feels a strong sense of intimate connection with another human being at that moment, even though the experience is over in a flash and even though the woman may be just a photographic image.

For a lonely, disconnected man, the sense of manhood and intimate connection are extremely potent draws, which explains why pornography and masturbation shine like a pan of fool's gold to his eyes. What a single guy can't get—the true intimacy from a real sexual encounter with a real woman—he can feel as if he's getting from the ejaculations of masturbation, because it provides many of the same feelings. What's more, even if he's feeling lonely and disconnected from guys, pornography and masturbation can still seem to fill the bill.

That's why I've said masturbation can be more of an emotional issue than a sexual one, and that's why you can stay hooked on masturbation long after you've given up the porn. You see, masturbation isn't just filling *sexual* holes in your life; it's also filling *emotional* holes—sometimes gaping ones. When you feel disconnected, self-stimulation becomes your escape, the medicating drug of choice, and in some ways it's better than drugs or alcohol, because an orgasm does more than get you high. It feels like real intimacy, if only for a moment.

When loneliness, discouragement, and disconnection leave you gasping for true intimacy in your life, the door is wide open for Satan to tempt you to seek this false intimacy with your own hands rather than seek genuine intimacy with God and with others. Now you can begin to understand why walking Christ's line of purity too loosely doesn't affect just *your* purity but also the purity of those around you. The spreading division and disconnection make it harder for everyone to stay pure.

You can also see why it is dangerous for a leader to teach, "Gang, you can watch anything you like as long as you don't feel bad about it yourself. If you don't feel bad about it in your heart, God must be okay with it in your life." That's a cop-out and far too simplistic. After all, your personal convictions and your views of purity are not just an issue in your life as a Christian; your decisions and your mediocrity can trip up your brothers on their walk with God too.

You must be diligent to find and teach God's line so that you can protect and promote the kind of emotional connection that helps you defend your sexual purity. It's part of your second great destiny and call:

> And the second is like it: "Love your neighbor as yourself." All the
> Law and the Prophets hang on these two commandments. (Matthew
> 22:39–40)

> A new command I give you: Love one another. As I have loved you, so
> you must love one another. By this all men will know that you are my
> disciples, if you love one another. (John 13:34–35)

In light of this great call, let's think back again on Brian's words from chapter 5: "My friends attack me because I find fault in almost everything currently on television or movies. I desperately want direction and guidance in my life on this." Brian was getting confused and frustrated, and he felt isolated and alone, even when standing among his brothers in Christ.

Now recall the harsh criticism that was dished Jasen's way by his Christian friends at college: *You're so narrow minded! We're free to watch whatever we want.* Do you suppose Jasen felt "one" with those guys? Do you suppose any of the non-Christian folks living on Jasen's dorm floor would have been impressed by the love these friends had for Jasen? Pretty doubtful.

Because of their soft knowledge of Scripture and a sloppy understanding of God's ways, these peers hammered and marginalized two guys who were hungry for God. That's wrong on principle alone, but it is quite deadly on the purity battlefield.

Think about it. If the Holy Spirit convicts your brother to cut back hard on the sensuality in his life, but then you isolate him because he's a "dud" and he won't go to the same movies anymore, does that isolation make it easier or harder for him to win his battle with porn and masturbation? Obviously, it will make it harder for him, and you must understand this if you ever expect to live normally as a Christian and answer your call from God to love your neighbors.

Perhaps you thought your battle for purity on the spiritual front would start and stop with the spiritual disciplines like prayer, worship, and fasting, but now you can see why it doesn't. It's not just your *vertical* relationship with God that matters when it comes to your purity—that is, loving God with all of your heart, soul, mind, and strength. Your *horizontal* relationships with your brothers will *also* matter deeply because of that tie between your interpersonal intimacy and your sexuality.

If you expect to win on the spiritual front of the battle and put your struggle to rest for good, you will need to know how your relationships with God and with others impact your ability to stand as a pure man in this day. Fulfilling the Great Commandment is central to your total victory.

Let me clarify something by asking you a few questions. Do you see God primarily as a king, commanding you to toe His lines and to curry His favor? Or do you see Him as a Father, firmly but graciously drawing you back to normal? If you have the right understanding of who God is and of the love He has for you, then the battle for purity will change dramatically.

What about that love for your neighbor? Do you have your brother's back in this battle despite the cost to you socially, or are you angry that his standards are tighter than yours, because it crimps your style? Is your heart filled with sadness and compassion for your brother's scriptural blindness, or are you bitter because he has *looser* standards than yours, for which you are now paying a heavier price socially? If you love your neighbor as yourself in this battle, the battle for purity will go much easier for each of you. If not, your sexual habits can spiral wildly out of control.

For Personal Reflection

1. In your own words, define the second main vulnerability in a guy's sexuality.
2. Why can't God just let the issue of your viewing habits slide?
3. Which vulnerability do you defend on the physical front of the battle? Which on the spiritual front?
4. Explain how a guy can remain hooked on masturbation even after he's dropped the porn.
5. True or false: Your vertical relationship with God is the only thing that matters on the spiritual front of the battle. Why or why not?

8

Cold Hearts, Cold Spirals

The Enemy uses the colder hearts of other Christians to discourage you in your fight for purity. The encouragement of your brothers and sisters in Christ should be a good line of defense in your battle for purity—*if* they're being obedient to God's laws and looking for ways to strengthen you and cheer you on when you take steps closer to Christ. This scripture says it well:

> See to it, brothers, that none of you has a sinful, unbelieving heart that turns away from the living God. But encourage one another daily, as long as it is called Today, so that none of you may be hardened by sin's deceitfulness. (Hebrews 3:12–13)

But when that encouragement is not there, sin's deceitfulness stabs away at your heart. Haunting questions will leave you with awful choices. *Should I back off on the physical front of the battle and just go back to the way I was so that I can fit in? Or do I persevere in guarding my eyes tightly and take the hits to my social life?*

As you contemplate what to do, discouragement often wiggles in through the door. You wonder, *Why am I living so tightly? Is it really doing me any good? I seemed happier before!* Now Satan has you right where he wants you; he knows that discouragement and disconnection from your friends trap you in masturbation's power.

Many hurting guys seek intimacy—any kind of intimacy—in the arms of a girlfriend, but that's not always possible. So who stands as the next best bet for scoring that feeling of intimacy and acceptance? If you said the nude women of the Net, you're right.

Too Much Pressure

On the World Wide Web there's an unlimited supply of playful women hoping to capture your eyes and mind, and this pixel harem is always available. So you check them out...and keep checking them out, hour after hour, because their pouty lips reveal that they understand your pain. They seem to know that a guy can only take so much wounding pressure.

That pressure pushes in from all directions, like when your friends drop you from their activities or you feel like a fifth wheel when you hang out with them. Pressure comes when you're stressed that you might lose your starting spot after a bad week of practice, so you turn in early for that relaxing jolt an orgasm delivers. It comes when your girlfriend toys with your emotions, hissing one moment that she wants to break up with you and purring the next that she wants you to hug her and hold her close. Masturbation puts you back in control again. It's your show of force—proof that you're a man who can handle things with women.

And so, in the end, masturbation binds you with a set of double chains. It's not only *physically* addictive because it provides a warm chemical bath for your brain's pleasure centers, but it's also *emotionally* addictive since it soothes stress and feels like balm for your sensitive wounds.

Perhaps you've been wounded while hacking your way through school life. It doesn't take much to get hurt and disconnected at school. Maybe the girls don't give you the time of day because you don't have the look they go for. Or the guys ignore you because you're timid and hang in the shadows. Or your ride isn't hot, your clothes aren't cool, and you don't shine in drama or sports.

The desire to connect with *anybody* can drive you into the arms of the cyberspace brothel. Maybe the real girls don't notice you, but the pretend ones do, and pretty soon you'll find yourself believing what Kyle does. He said, "I've learned that online porn and masturbation offer the 'gentle stroking' that we males need. I can tell you this: it's better than nothing."

The trouble with Kyle's tack is that masturbation is an implosion of sexual pleasure that focuses a guy further and further into himself. That "gentle stroking" *isn't* what we males need, because it doesn't connect you to the world around you. In fact, it disconnects you.

Kellen knows that too well. He wrote me to say that he was known as the big fat kid who anybody at school could go to with a computer question. He was a computer nerd who didn't have many friends.

It wasn't long before I was shutting myself out from the world for days
on end after school, downloading sexy pictures to feed my mind for
hours and hours. Those pics filled my mind constantly during class as
I daydreamed about everything I saw the night before.

Kyle claimed the "gentle stroking" of masturbation was better than nothing, but Kellen discovered the truth: it was *much worse* than nothing. You see, the genuine need a guy has for intimacy cannot be met by self-seeking sexual activity. Your original itch for intimacy can't be scratched or satisfied by porn and masturbation; it only feels that way for a fleeting moment. In the end, though, your heart is left itching, and all you can do is head back to the computer for some more gentle stroking, which drives you further within yourself, which leaves you itching and feeling emptier. And so the downward spiral goes.

If you get caught up in Internet porn like Kellen, you'll be like a dog chasing his tail. The cycle will be endless. Once you turn inward and fixate on porn and masturbation—and yourself—your problems only compound as your sense of disconnection deepens.

Secondary Effects

The spiral of masturbation can be awful to break, but a second, vicious spiral may spin into your life as well, even *after* you've made your stand against it. When you're standing alone in the battle and finding yourself paying heavier and heavier social prices, it's too easy to let your eyes slip off the Lord's will and purposes in your life and become angry or jealous over those who are taking their fill of free love and unbridled sex. As the divisions run their course and your frustrations reach critical mass, you'll sometimes pick up an abnormal, myopic view of the world and of all the sinners around you, Christian or otherwise.

They seem to have it all, and soon you're talking like Jim, who, after reading *Every Young Man's Battle,* wrote: "You must have been quite a ladies' man, Fred. I went to school with a lot of guys like you, but they were never my friends because I had no respect for them. They were nothing but arrogant, egotistical, self-centered jerks who only loved themselves and treated the girls like dirt. When I look back now, though, perhaps I was jealous of them."

I'm glad Jim told me how he really feels, but I was struck by how his words sounded like Asaph's frustrating, moping testimony in the Old Testament:

> But as for me, my feet had almost slipped;
>> I had nearly lost my foothold.
> For I envied the arrogant....

> Surely in vain have I kept my heart pure;
>> in vain have I washed my hands in innocence....

> When I tried to understand all this,
>> it was oppressive to me

till I entered the sanctuary of God;
    then I understood their final destiny. (Psalm 73:2–3, 13, 16–17)

Asaph felt sorry for himself, but to his credit, he also recognized what this outside focus had done to his senses:

When my heart was grieved
    and my spirit embittered,
I was senseless and ignorant;
    I was a brute beast before you. (Psalm 73:21–22)

Jim had slipped into this same state of affairs regarding the godless guys around him—guys like I was. His thoughts had become brutish and angry toward them, but in reality, those feelings made little sense in two ways. First, anger only leads to more disconnection, and that's the last thing any guy needs in his battle for purity. But second, once you've fallen into this pattern of jealousy and anger, you'll find that any effort to become more normal and pure in your sexuality will leave this nasty little side effect in your soul: you'll become *less* normal in the way you view the people around you. How so? Let me explain.

We are to have the full mind of Christ, right? If God loved you while you were still a sinner, aren't you supposed to do the same with others? Even if you can't quite manage to love them yet, shouldn't you at least have pity for them? You would if you had the mind of Christ. Jesus *always* has compassion for each and every one:

When he saw the crowds, he had compassion on them, because they were harassed and helpless, like sheep without a shepherd. (Matthew 9:36)

If you aren't careful to keep your eyes on the Lord and off the actions of the lost, you can pick up a narrower view that blinds you and makes you forget something that no Christian should ever forget: sin destroys, and God cannot be mocked. Any man stuck in a cesspool of sexual sin, as I was, should be greatly pitied, not envied or scorned. That man is dying inside.

Jim had clearly become blind like that. He was certain I was in love with myself, an arrogant, egotistical, self-centered jerk. Was his assessment of my life accurate? Not even remotely. If he'd had the mind of Christ, he would have been thinking normally and compassionately, like Jesus, and he would have known that my wounds were tearing me apart inside, no matter how things looked on the surface. Take a peek at this entry from my journal, written near the end of my sophomore year at Stanford:

> I want to be free from Dad's power over me. I can barely stand living under the pressure of all his opinions about me any longer.
>
> I feel like I live in a world of others, a world in which I don't actually exist. My inferiority complex encompasses me—everything I think and say seems unimportant, and every last thing that anyone else says is true and significant. I feel I'm hardly ever funny anymore because my mind is too bogged down with self-consciousness to do anything but worry. I rarely contribute to the conversations at the dorm dinner tables, and I rarely smile, because it's hard to enjoy the present when you're so worried about whether the other guy is enjoy- ing his present with you. I can't even enjoy my girlfriend because I'm playing so many manipulative games of self-protection instead of communicating with her.
>
> I'd like to think I'm improving, because those month-long low moods are getting shorter, and my happier moods are lasting longer now. But the truth is, those social pains and fears are still overwhelming to me, and that longing for death still grips my mind far too often.

Remember, sin grinds slowly, but it always grinds true. It's easy to forget this once your eyes slip off the truth of the Word and focus upon the carefree, "happier" lives of others around you.

But the Word is always true, and it was playing out perfectly in my life. I could not free myself from the porn and masturbation, which clung to me like tentacles. Sick of the money spent on full-color flesh magazines and sick of the wasted time looking at this stuff, half of me tried to peel off their muscular grip. But the other half of me kept wrapping the tentacles back around my penis, whining, *How can we live without our friends?*

And when it came to real women, I was faring no better. Harassed to distraction by my sin, I found it harder and harder to successfully juggle the demands of four girlfriends. All the "connecting" I did late at night left me feeling as though I wasn't connected to anything—even to these women. How could this be? All I knew was that I felt like a gerbil on a wheel, running faster and faster, but spinning nowhere fast. In spite of all the sex, I was lonely, bone-crushingly lonely.

Sensuality's Chains Return

So where will all this looking around at your peers take you? Absolutely nowhere. In fact, your last state may be worse than your first. Take a look at the pattern.

In the beginning, your wounds and disconnection drove you toward pornography and masturbation as a medication for your pain, which eventually warped your view of women. So to straighten out your view of women, you tried to give up the disconnection of porn and masturbation, only to pick up deep discouragement with your brothers in Christ because of their hypocritical lifestyles (as I pointed out in chapter 6). Or maybe you're jealous regarding the carefree lifestyles of the unsaved (as Jim was).

In the end, you've simply stepped out of sensuality's chains and into a new pair of chains labeled "Spiritual Pride" and "Anger," leaving you no better off as a Christian than when you began. Worse yet, that new, jealous, angry attitude of yours will likely add to the discouraging disconnection you've been feeling around your friends, and it may even drop you back into the chains of porn and masturbation as well. You simply can't afford this bitter spiral of emotions.

Where Victory Begins

If you expect to find a place of victory and transformation, Scripture ordains a clear plan:

> Therefore, since we are surrounded by such a great cloud of witnesses, let us throw off everything that hinders and the sin that so easily entangles, and let us run with perseverance the race marked out for us. *Let us fix our eyes on Jesus, the author and perfecter of our faith.* (Hebrews 12:1–2)

If you desire to persevere in the race for purity that has been marked out for you, it's not enough to throw off everything that hinders and the sin that so easily entangles—the eye candy, the porn, the sexy television shows. You must also keep your eyes fixed upon Jesus, the Living Word.

When you fix your eyes on anything but Jesus, you quickly get into trouble. The perfecting of your faith is slower, and the transformation of your mind is halted. Another scripture alludes to the danger here:

> When they measure themselves by themselves and compare themselves with themselves, they are not wise. (2 Corinthians 10:12)

These two scriptures hint at how easily you can be blinded in this battle for purity. If you started strongly in the battle and then faded as the costs got higher and your emotions spiraled downward, it could also explain why you don't own the field yet.

If you feel connected and accepted by those around you, you'll have plenty of true intimacy in your life. You won't need the false intimacy of porn and masturbation to make up for what's missing. A close, tight intimacy with the Father also replaces that need for false intimacy because you can have all the intimacy you need through Him.

That's why it's important to do everything you can to keep your relationship with your brothers healthy and your relationship with God strong. Now, some young people have been wounded by their earthly fathers, which has created a spiral of pain that prevents them from connecting effectively with their heavenly Father. This disconnection from the Father surely impacts the battle for purity, and I'll discuss how these "father wounds" affect us in the next chapter.

For Personal Reflection

1. Ponder these questions again from page 91: Do you see God primarily as a king, commanding you to toe His lines and to curry His favor? Or do you see Him as a Father, firmly but graciously drawing you back to normal? Do you have your brother's back in this battle despite the cost to you socially, or are you angry that his tighter standards crimp your style? Is your heart filled with sadness and compassion for your brother's scriptural blindness, or are you bitter because his looser standards force you to pay a heavier social price?

2. How does masturbation bind you with two types of chains?

3. Why is masturbation worse than nothing?

4. How can anger toward your brother in Christ feed a masturbation habit?

9

Father Wounds

The wounds that drive us toward masturbation can assault us from anywhere, but the broadest, most jagged ones come from our fathers. When I played high-school football, I played for an audience of one. Sure there were thousands of people in the stands—Friday-night high-school football is big stuff in the heartland—but only one voice mattered during the game: the leather-lunged outbursts from my father.

"Get your head up!" he'd yell from behind our bench whenever I fumbled a snap or missed a receiver. Throwing an interception earned a stronger rebuke: "Get your head out of your rear," he'd scream, except that he didn't use the word *rear.*

I feared Dad's verbal blitzes more than the linebackers blitzing on my blind side. He'd wait for me after the game and then walk me to the car as he kept up a fiery, nonstop discourse about how I shouldn't have overthrown a receiver in the end zone or should have hit a different hole when I ran the ball. His criticisms upset me so much that one time I threw up into my ball cap.

He'd drop by and do the same thing at practice too. In our huddles, my teammates mentioned how bad they felt for me and how they wished he'd just go home. Nothing I could do, nothing I could say was good enough for my father. I had this hole in my heart because I never felt like I measured up as a man, no matter how much the other players respected me.

This was no ordinary wound. There was a gaping hole of inadequacy that left me feeling lonely and cut off from the rest of the world. That's one reason why I went looking for love—and my manhood—elsewhere. I found it in bed with young women. Remember what I said about the primary way that guys give and receive intimacy? It's in the things we do with a woman prior to and during sexual intercourse.

The deepest wound my dad inflicted on me was his divorce. Many guys are driven to masturbation after the train wreck of their parents' divorce, which should surprise no one. After all, masturbation is a handy way to salve insecurity or psychological pain, and nothing delivers a load of pain quite like the divorce of your parents. It's far easier to run to the computer with a jar of Vaseline than cope with a trauma like this in a healthy, interactive way.

Sean wrote this to me:

> The past two semesters I've been chairman of the largest Christian group on campus, but winter break brought on some rough weeks. My parents broke up this past semester and left Ma bankrupt, so no more cable. That should have helped me in the battle, but that first night home, I found the cutest girl on one of our four channels and masturbated anyway. The next couple of weeks leading up to the New Year were filled with lust and masturbation like I haven't experienced since high school.

The splintering effects of your parents' divorce (or parental death) will shatter your world, causing great internal anguish, anger, and insecurity. Despite all their talk about how they're doing the right thing, you feel robbed and even cast aside, left to seek intimacy wherever you can find it.

Patrick Middleton, a good friend and a marvelous counselor specializing in addictions, knows all about these intimacy issues. Recently he told me:

> I deal with a lot of adult men, and it never fails that the men with the deeper sexual issues also have uninvolved or missing fathers. Their sex-

ual issues are directly and severely impacted by their dad's failures as a father.

Why is that? Because there's a point in the development of a boy into a man—usually between ages eleven and thirteen—when a boy needs to move into a deeper relationship with his father. Patrick continued:

> I know this sounds a bit weird, but I've never found a better way to
> say it: dad has to be close enough to his son to be able to call the "heart
> of the man" out of the boy. If this does not happen, the next window
> of opportunity for a young man to try to feel like a man is through his
> emerging sexuality. So if Dad isn't there early in adolescence to help
> answer questions about manhood, the boy will use his sexuality to
> answer his questions about being a man.

When it comes to searching out your identity, receiving a real man's insight and stamp of approval is everything. You need a father or important man in your life to put an arm around your shoulder and tell you that you're okay. When it comes to your sexuality, you need him to say that you can ask him anything you want about sex: wet dreams, masturbation, sexual temptation, the tight tops on the girls in the weightroom, the whole nine yards. And when it comes to the rest of your life, you need him to answer your questions about what works in life and what doesn't, what makes for success, and what is worth pouring your life into. Without this fatherly input, things can unravel quickly when it comes to sexual purity.

My dad wasn't there for me when I wanted to ask those questions, so I was left to sort out my manhood by paging through porn magazines and touching willing women. Needless to say, that approach worked out miserably for me, and the reason was elementary: men become men in the company of men, not in the company of women.

I was the only guy left in the house after Dad slammed the front door on his way out. Sure, Mom told me endlessly that I was becoming a fine man, and my two older sisters said plenty of girls thought I was one handsome hunk of burliness. Girls at school called me foxy and cute.

But no matter how often they said these nice things, they didn't count. Only another man can declare you a man. "You fit in, boy. Come on up and stand with us, shoulder to shoulder." And if the man saying this is your father, it's a hundred times better.

With fathers leaving their families by the millions, however, countless young guys are left behind to hack their way on their own through puberty and into manhood. Without that connection with your father and his acceptance of you as a man, because of your sexual makeup, you are at great risk of falling into sexual sin during your teen and young adult years. If orgasmic relief becomes a crutch in your wounded and crippled life, you'll drag that crutch into your adult years.

No Time for Silence

Even if your father sleeps right down the hall, watches football games with you every weekend, and buys you a Ford pickup, he still hasn't given you everything you need if he's been silent about your emerging sexuality. More often than not, you'll wind up searching for manhood through your sexuality. Jordan had this to say:

> My dad wasn't good at showing love at home, and kids made fun of me every day at school, so I was empty and needy. So I often felt I needed to look at a woman's naked body to get an erection just so I could feel manly. It felt like I needed to prove something to myself, and even to that woman on the screen. Why did I have to prove something to her? She was just a picture—go figure!

I'm not here to knock fathers. Being a father is the most difficult thing I've ever done. I'll never forget watching my first child, Jasen, slide into the world. The doctor caught him, slapped him across the rear, toweled him off brusquely, and stretched a goofy little hat over his head to keep him warm. Then, as the nurse delivered this moist little bundle into my arms, I felt a weight settle on my shoulders: the responsibility for the physical, emotional, and spiritual nourishment of an eternal soul.

I wasn't remotely equipped for fatherhood. What did I know? After all, my father left home when I was in elementary school. I had no idea what a father should do about raising a boy. Nor had I grown up hearing heroic stories about my forefathers building business empires or fighting in far-off lands. The stories I'd heard were the kind that adults whispered. For instance, my grandfather—my father's father—had deserted his family in the middle of the Great Depression; my father didn't see him again until he became a father himself. How, then, could my father have known what it meant to be a good dad?

I believe my father meant to do a good job of raising me, and I'm sure he loved me. I'm also sure he thought that bellowing at me at Friday-night football games or showing me his *Playboys* was the best way to make a man out of me. Too bad he didn't know he was hurting, not helping, me.

But that's key to what I want you to understand. It is very, very easy for fathers to be inept at what they do. That's one reason I eventually chose to show mercy to Dad, and in the latter years of his life, we built a relationship that we could both enjoy. But that's also why a loving dad can still wound you deeply, even though he thinks he's helping you, as Keith learned:

> When I was twelve, I had a particularly bad teacher who failed our whole class. She was so bad that the school fired her the following year, but the damage was done. My dad pulled me out of public school to homeschool me.
>
> Suddenly I had no social life, but I thought I had the answer to that loneliness—masturbation. Two years later I'm trapped in this and can't get out.

Or, feeling the weight of the responsibility to raise you well, a father may panic in crunch time, as Jeffrey attested in this letter to me:

Last New Year's Day I was at a party with the youth group when I began conversing with this girl that I'd been interested in for a long time. As we talked, I discovered that she liked me too. Before long, we were exchanging love letters without the knowledge of my parents. Three weeks later my dad found out about her on a Sunday morning. I was already at church, but he called me on my cell and told me to meet him outside. After Dad picked me up, he commenced a seven-hour-long, mostly one-way conversation about why she wasn't right for me.

Seven hours! I was extremely hurt emotionally, and I just kind of closed up. I went for weeks without talking to my friends, and I stopped going to youth group. I stopped doing schoolwork and started looking at porn all day long. And any time this girl came to my mind, I cried.

If you've had a rocky time with your father, join the club. I certainly know what it's like, and if you're like me, his wounding behavior may have fueled your drive into pornography and masturbation.

But please don't miss my point here. This isn't about your father, the ways he failed you, or the things he should have taught you about sexuality and manhood. He was who he was then, and he is who he is now.

But so are you, and that's the point you need to focus on. No matter how you got here, you are who you are today. If that picture includes wounds and disconnection, then there's a good chance you have an emotional dependence upon masturbation. Keeping an angry heart toward your father and dwelling on his mistakes won't help you; it'll only fuel more disconnection. Given your sexual vulnerabilities, that's a luxury you can't afford in the battle. You need to forgive and move on for your own good.

Still, we need to discuss these father wounds for a good reason. If you've got them, you've likely been sorting out your manhood through your sexuality as I did, and by now you probably have a skewed, abnormal view of what it means to be a man. A transformation of your mind is in order. You need to recognize these father wounds for what they are and understand how they affect your battle for sexual purity.

This isn't about your father; it's about you and how these father wounds are affecting your view of your heavenly Father.

Enjoying a Good Steak

I came to the realization that *my* wounds had affected my view of the heavenly Father during a road trip that started when I climbed wearily onto a bus with forty-four guys one July evening at midnight. After the driver fired up the engine, we rolled in the darkness toward Boulder, Colorado, for a stadium-style, two-day Christian seminar for guys on the University of Colorado campus.

Greg Laurie, a Southern California evangelist and the man behind the Harvest Crusades, opened things up on Friday evening with a salvation message. While I'd been saved years ago, I was still struggling with deep issues regarding my relationship with my domineering father. The lack of my father's acceptance had been rocking me hard, and these old wounds were severely affecting my relationship with my wife and kids through my angry temper. I needed some answers badly.

In the middle of his talk, Greg mentioned that our achievements do not impress God, because He is behind them all anyway. "God doesn't arch His eyebrows and give a low whistle when He sees that I am the pastor of a church with ten thousand members," he said. "It doesn't impress Him that I'm on stage right now talking to fifty thousand men. He doesn't really need that from me; He could use anyone. When it comes to our relationship together, it doesn't matter to Him whether I'm successful or not. The same goes for each of you out there."

Then Greg paused for a moment before making a simple statement that blew me away. "The truth is, all God wants is to put His arm around you and have a steak with you." Instantly God's revelation crashed through my spirit like a meteor.

God wants to put His arm around me and cut into a juicy steak with me? I know Greg's word picture sounded absurdly simple, but when his words mixed with God's power in my spirit, years of pain, agony, and frustration over my dad crumbled into dust. Unlike my father down here, my heavenly Father already saw me as His son. I didn't have to prove myself. I had real value. He didn't care a thing about what I achieved or what I did or if I was successful. All He wanted was a chance to sit down with me, wrap His arm around me, and cut into a barbecued steak with me!

Until that night, I wasn't aware that I didn't know God as Father. I knew Him quite well as King and feared Him deeply as Lord. But I had never really known Him as my Daddy.

If I could choose just one thing for you to take away from reading this book, it would be the revelation of God as your Father—your Abba, your Daddy. Once you have that, the battle for purity changes forever.

Forget everything else for a moment. Forget your addictions, forget your poor relationship with your father, and forget your computer that keeps calling you over to take a peek. Forget all of it. Focus on this one thing: *Your Enemy wants to keep you in your place, but the Father wants to free you to fly. It's time to turn to Him and get to know your Dad.*

Too often guys have the wrong goal on this spiritual front of the battle. They want instant deliverance, here and now. But the real objective on this spiritual front is genuine intimacy, both with God and with others. True intimacy *will* deliver you in this battle, and true intimacy with the Father is where the transformation of your heart begins.

So many guys pour all of their energy into accountability relationships with their friends, sure that they need extra sets of eyes looking over their shoulders to keep them honest. Who's to argue? That kind of accountability is a wonderful tool and something we'll discuss later.

Still, what most guys need even more is a genuine *connection.* Connection is not so much about accountability as it is about intimacy. You see, it's not the extra set of eyes that gives connection its power; it's the intimacy itself.

Most men aren't falling because they don't have enough peer pressure in their lives. They are falling because they don't have enough true intimacy and connection in their lives. So they seek the false intimacy of porn and mastur-bation to make up for that lack. Peer pressure can't satisfy that hunger for intimacy, and so while it is wise to have this kind of accountability with your friends, by itself it can never quite reach the root of the problem.

Genuine intimacy can, however, and that's why the best way to get over your dependence on false intimacy is to replace it with the real thing. God knows that, and He will never stop working with you until you have the intimacy with Him necessary to end the battle. He wants to live with you and fight the root of the problem with you.

Genuine intimacy and friendship with God defends that crucial sexual vulnerability as no person on earth can. Unlike your pals, God is never on vacation in the Caribbean or out for pizza when you desperately need to talk to somebody. The Father's phone never goes to voice mail when you call; He's as close as the mention of His name.

Because of that, you need to pour as much energy into your accountability relationship with God as you would with anyone else. My Father and I have grown to enjoy a wonderful intimacy since that weekend in Colorado. When I walk outside in the morning, I'm absolutely certain that I'm walking with the Lord and that the Enemy jumps to the alert. When I'm at my computer during the day, His presence with me is as real as mine is. My limits as a man to choose my own way are crystal clear now. My whole mind has been transformed through the washing of the Word, and my sexuality has been redeemed through this never-ending intimacy with Him.

In a real sense, very little has changed since high school when I played before an audience of one—my hard-charging father—though there were thousands of others cheering away. Today I simply have a *new* audience of One, and while there may still be thousands around me screaming their thoughts about my play on His field, I only hear my Father, and I only see His Son.

He has perfected my game as my relationship with Him has deepened, and that's where your victory over sexual sin will be completed too. It's in that relationship with Him where the transformation of your mind truly happens, and it's there you can finally settle your identity as a man.

Remember, your Father not only wants to bring your eyes and your sexuality back to normal, but He also wants to bring your dependencies back to normal. He wants your eyes looking straight ahead at Him, not at the women, not at your wounds, and not at all the sinners out there having fun. He wants you depending upon Him, not upon a jar of Vaseline.

In the Bible, Asaph had his eyes looking everywhere but up. Once he slipped into sin through his jealousy, he had to start all over again, turning his whole heart and both eyes toward his Father. When he did so, he found a deep intimacy and connection that would keep his feet from slipping again:

> Yet I am always with you;
>> you hold me by my right hand.
> You guide me with your counsel,
>> and afterward you will take me into glory. (Psalm 73:23–24)

Where do *you* go to start over once *your* feet slip? The answer: the same place Asaph did—to the heart of our Father. That intimacy keeps your feet from slipping again.

Of course, amid the silence and failures of our earthly fathers, it can be difficult to get a clear picture of what the Father's heart is like toward His sons, so it may be hard to believe you can have such intimacy with Him. But you can, and no matter how badly your earthly dad botched things up for you, I think you can catch this picture of an intimate Father if we work on it together. After all, Greg Laurie did that for me. Now I want to do the same for you.

I want to paint a picture of a father's heart for his son so you can understand just how passionate your heavenly Dad's heart is for you in this battle. I can't overstate how critical this is for you. Recall what I said earlier: *If I could choose just one thing for you to take away from reading this book, it would be the revelation of God as your Father—your Abba, your Daddy. Once you have that, the battle for purity changes forever.*

I'd choose this one thing because I know from experience that His love is at the root of your destiny:

And I pray that you, being rooted and established in love, may have power…to grasp how wide and long and high and deep is the love of Christ, and to know this love that surpasses knowledge—that you may be filled to the measure of all the fullness of God…who is able to do immeasurably more than all we ask or imagine, according to his power that is at work within us. (Ephesians 3:17–20)

Long-term purity starts with walking in God's *ways* on the *physical* front of the battle and is completed by walking in God's *love* on the *spiritual* front. Sexual purity needn't be a lifelong, white-knuckle solo flight. Once you know Him as your Father, the battle changes forever. Intimacy invades every corner of your life and relationships, and victory is at hand. Purity becomes easy once you find that conscious sense of His genuine love for you.

Perhaps that's still hard to believe and you're moaning, *I know in my head that God loves me, but on a day-to-day basis I just don't see myself that way.*

Then it's time to turn to Him and get to know your Dad. I'll help you do that over the next three chapters.

For Personal Reflection

1. When it comes to your earthly dad, do you sense his acceptance of you as a man? Has he told you that you fit out there in the world of men, right at his side?

2. Has your father been around to help you sort through manhood and answer your questions about sexuality, or have you been left to sort through it on your own? How has that affected your life in relation to porn and to girls? Has it suddenly helped you connect some dots in your life?

3. *If I could choose just one thing for you to take away from reading this book, it would be the revelation of God as your Father—your Abba, your Daddy.* Why do you suppose this revelation can change your battle for purity forever?

YOU AND YOUR FATHER

We live in what some call a "fatherless generation." Tonight in the United States, 40 percent of all children will go to bed in different homes than their fathers. When I speak at colleges and youth retreats and ask guys one-on-one what their relationship is like with their father, I almost never see a smile. I see stricken faces, rolled eyes, deep frowns, long scowls, and pooling tears, but I rarely see a warm smile. What's more, after decades of runaway divorce rates in this country, many adults feel the weight of what some have called the "orphan spirit." In a sentence, they describe it this way: "Yes, I have a father, but I never felt fathered."

If that's you, perhaps you're confused when you crack open the Bible and find God saying: "'Therefore come out from them and be separate, says the Lord....' 'I will be a Father to you, and you will be my sons and daughters, says the Lord Almighty'" (2 Corinthians 6:17–18).

God is clearly excited about the offer He's made here, but if you've come from a bent or broken home, this may not seem like much of a deal. *My dad called me filthy names and cursed me if I didn't do things exactly his way. Who needs another father?*

Your heavenly Father has a good reason for being excited. He knows what a normal father looks like, and He knows how you'll blossom when He starts fathering you normally. And that brings us to an important turning point in this book. From here on, I'll be teaching you how to reach out and connect with this Father and with those around you so that you can win decisively on the spiritual front of this battle.

But let me be very blunt from the start. This can *also* be a turning point in your *life,* if you want it to be. You once humbled yourself and risked looking silly when you chose to starve your sumo on the physical front of the battle. Now you must choose to risk again, this time risking friendship and intimacy with God and others. I know this may feel like a huge risk, just as it did for me at the start.

But once you've taken a hard look at your sexual vulnerabilities, you'll see that it's an even *bigger* risk to believe the Enemy's lies and to sit around crying, *I ain't no good. Nobody likes me. God won't reach back toward a nothing like me!* That's a guaranteed sack, and believing such lies is a luxury you can't afford on this field. Isn't it time to see yourself for who you really are and to actually live like it for a change? You'll have to do it sometime. Why not now?

You are a son of God. You are worthy. Risk broadly and be disciplined about it. Reach out to Him and to others. Sure, you'll get burned along the way, just as we all do. But whenever it happens, stand up and risk again. Seek connection with all your heart, because your purity depends upon it. Remember, your destiny is at hand.

In the midst of this fatherless generation, you may have been playing the field with the coeds at school—or at least the babes in cyberspace. That's in the past. God wants you to stop playing the field and to start owning it instead, playing for an audience of One.

Let's see exactly who this One is who has asked us to separate ourselves and be His children.

10

A Father's Heart

It took more than a decade as a Christian before I finally understood my Father's love for me—that I'm His boy, and that's all that matters.

Of course, He loved me even before I knew Him, and He's desired to be with me from the foundation of the world. I never did a thing to fan that desire in His heart, and I'll never have to, either. When I couldn't put my porn away, He still loved me. When I fell into the arms of too many women, He still loved me. My Father adopted me, and now I'm the apple of His eye. He has opened up His heart to me forever, just as He's opened it up to you. Your sin can't separate you from His love, because Jesus paid the penalty for your sin years ago:

> My dear children, I write this to you so that you will not sin. But
> if anybody does sin, we have one who speaks to the Father in our
> defense—Jesus Christ, the Righteous One. He is the atoning sacrifice
> for our sins, and not only for ours but also for the sins of the whole
> world. (1 John 2:1–2)

His love for you and His plan to save you have been in place from before the dawn of time. His passion to explore life with you will stretch to eternity. Nothing you ever did ignited this love for you, and nothing you'll ever do will kill it. He is your Father. You are His son.

Until your mind is transformed concerning the spiritual front of your battle for purity, you're doomed to see your Father as another finger-pointing accuser standing against you. If so, you'll never win the battle because seeing your Father as an accuser increases your feelings of disconnection and pummels your sexual vulnerabilities.

That truth was hammered home to me once again by this painful e-mail from a mother whose son was in the throes of a major battle:

> My son is a political science major at a Bible college out west, and he is an amazingly gifted athlete, writer, and speaker. He's also engaged to marry a sweet, pure girl, and they have both vowed their deep love and purity toward one another.
>
> This seemingly perfect son revealed to my husband and me this spring that he had been secretly masturbating since he was about fourteen, and he has admitted that since the engagement, his masturbation has increased dramatically. This leaves us in a big dilemma because we believe he is suffering from clinical depression and an anxiety disorder over his guilt. From our distant vantage point, he is exhibiting the classic symptoms of depression: lack of concentration, lack of sleep, obsessive behavior, and a loss of interest in things he loves to do.
>
> In fact, I would dare to call it a religious obsessive compulsion. Every time he phones home, all he wants to talk about is this problem, and he gauges the success or failure of his day by whether or not he masturbated.
>
> His behavior is beginning to rip at the seams of his relationship with his fiancée. In the interest of having an open relationship, he disclosed his problem with sexual purity to her. After doing so, though, his self-image fell into the basement, and now he feels unworthy of the girl he plans to marry. It only added fuel to that fire when she related his problem to her parents, because now they aren't so sure he's good for their daughter.

He is so flooded with guilt and shame that he even made another decision for salvation a few weeks ago, in spite of the fact that he's always been very conscientious about his walk with God. The oppressive atmosphere at his college is not helping this situation, as the school is extremely legalistic and places a high emphasis on chapel messages focusing on guilt and sin. We have talked to the dean of men about that focus on guilt, but all he did was say, "Your son needs to get into the Word."

My son is losing hope. On the phone with us, he uses phrases like, "I'm useless," "I'm hopeless," and "I'll never get victory over this." How do I get my son to see himself as a child of God, no longer living in condemnation?

I did my best to answer her last question with concepts in this chapter that I'm relating from my own experience. For me, it started with a living revelation regarding the truth of God delivered by Greg Laurie at Folsom Field and, more important, a revelation of the *heart* that lies behind that truth. It'll come to you the same way.

Looking for God's Heart

When God gave us His law and truth, He didn't intend for them to become a club we would use to beat ourselves over the head with forever:

> Indeed I would not have known what sin was except through the law.
> For I would not have known what coveting really was if the law had
> not said, "Do not covet." (Romans 7:7)

What was our Lord's heart in this? He clearly wanted us to know right from wrong, but why? Did He spell out the law to make sure that we would avoid hurting *Him,* or did He do it to protect us from hurting *ourselves*?

He did it to protect *us*! In His infinite wisdom, He knew the destructive nature of sin and what it means to be freed from its power. The law was given so we'd know how to avoid sin and eventually recognize our need for a Savior. He gave us the law out of love. To better understand our Father's heart behind His law, let me tell you a story about *my* heart and love as a father.

Jasen had my heart wrapped up from the moment I first saw him. His birth was like a bright sunrise in my life, so I gave him a pet nickname—Sun Boy—that is ours alone. No one uses it but me.

Every unique trait about him mesmerized me. Matchbox cars meant everything to him, and he always slept clutching one in his hand, especially his beloved "taxi-cabby car-car." He also had a thing for sticks. Jasen's first word wasn't "no" or "Mama," as it so often is with kids. His first utterance was "stick…stick," and a stroller ride just wasn't right unless he had a stick in his hand.

I captured Jasen's heart from the start too. When he'd hear my voice from his crib, he'd thrash about like a flopping fish. Later, when I'd come in from work, he'd toddle over to me on his spindly legs, grinning and drooling as he adoringly looked up into his hero's eyes in his wondrous, innocent way. All he wanted was to be with me, and though he couldn't talk yet, everything about his wide eyes and toothy smile yearned to tell me, *Daddy, you're everything to me. I want to be just like you someday.*

Most of the time my heart soared to see that little wet grin, but sometimes my heart broke and the tears poured after I looked into those big blue eyes. I was so afraid he actually would grow up and become like me that, in prayer, I'd literally moan out loud over his future. "Oh God," I'd beg, "isn't there any way to keep him out of this pit I'm in?"

The last thing I wanted for my innocent son was for him to get trapped by the same addictive porn habits of my grandpa, my dad, and finally, me. My sexuality owned me, and since I couldn't control it, I knew Jasen would soon be paying the same toll that many other men in my family had paid.

That thought gutted my soul mercilessly! I hated looking at myself in the mirror because of shame over my sexual sin. I felt a stark, hopeless desperation when I looked into Jasen's eyes. I had no hope and no insight. I had no way to show my son what it meant to live a pure life, and I had no clue how to lead him there.

Many mornings I would awake before dawn and mull this question over and over: *Why did God ever allow me to become a father of a son?* Sexual sin was practically a birthright in my family, and I had eagerly carried on the tradition when I was old enough to mess around with girls. What kind of role model could I be? As far as I was concerned, Jasen was doomed. What hope did he have to escape my family's generational patterns of sexual sin?

You can imagine the emotions I felt when I looked into this trusting boy's eyes and realized that his hero—me—would have to take responsibility for making sure the cords of sexual sin would never bind him.

A father's love for his son stirs up groans and tears like this, but it can also spur a man to engage the battle for purity. The father's heart inside me demanded that I win and demanded that I teach Jasen everything I'd learned in my battle, no matter how embarrassing it might seem. My heart insisted that I find a way out for Jasen, because if I didn't, I couldn't really say I loved him as much as I thought I did. I was his father, and a father's love *must* fight for his son's freedom. I had to sacrifice anything to get it for him.

It's this same kind of love that compelled God to lay down His Son's life to set you free and to give you His Word to help you know how to walk free. With one look into your eyes, His love was spurred to engage your battle. He'll never rest until you're completely free.

This was the heart behind His law from the beginning. It was born of a Father's loving heart that can't step away from you, whether you're winning or losing.

Powerful Stuff

When Jasen turned eleven, we spent a number of nights reading the book *Preparing for Adolescence* and sorting through the birds and the bees stuff together, including Dr. James Dobson's description of sexual intercourse. Man, what a wild ride!

We had a great time, and I wouldn't trade those memories for the world. On one of those evenings, it came time to share the effects of pornography with him. "Jace, looking at pictures of naked women is a lot like taking drugs," I declared.

Jasen looked at me quizzically. His fifth-grade mind didn't make the connection.

"Here's what I mean," I said. "When we look at women without clothes on, there is a chemical reaction in our brains that some say is much like the reaction the brain has to cocaine. I remember reading some studies about this way back when I was in college. I also remember seeing some of my rich Stanford friends blow thousands of dollars on cocaine over spring break. They kept snorting and snorting the stuff, and they couldn't get enough. It's like they couldn't stop."

"Wow," said my son, his eyes getting bigger.

"You got that right, Jace. But here's the thing. I never tried cocaine at Stanford, but I sure looked at pornography, and once I did, I was hooked just like those guys with their drugs. It took me years to break this brutal habit, Son, and I don't want you to make the same mistake I did."

"Sure, Dad."

We were fortunate to have had the conversation when we did, because two weeks later one of Jasen's friends brought a *Hustler* magazine to school. Between classes, he called all the guys over to peak at the glossy photos. Jasen came home and related what had happened at school, and given my background, I was already impressed that he was brave enough to tell me.

"So what did you do?" I asked.

"I walked away, just like you said I should."

My jaw dropped to my chest. *My son walked away from porn!* My heart sang and my feet felt like dancing. Jasen was the first Stoeker in four generations who had walked away from porn when it was offered to him. *Could this be the first crack in our generational wall?* We'd been imprisoned for decades! My mind was carried away by that thought for weeks.

But what if Jasen had failed? How would a normal father's heart respond to a son's defeat, or, more accurately, how *must* it respond? Before you answer that, think back to my passion and desperation as I looked into Jasen's eyes when he was a toddler. Imagine again my agony and tears for him. Consider my heart in warning him about porn in the first place.

Did I warn him about porn because I wanted to crimp his style and lord over my son? Heavens no! I was his father. It was all about keeping my precious Sun Boy out of prison, no matter what it cost me. Win or lose, I was committed for the duration of his battle. Jasen was and is my son. His freedom and my love cannot be separated in my heart.

That's why there is only one way for a father's heart to respond if his son fails. This is how a normal dad looks:

For you know that we dealt with each of you as a father deals with his own children, encouraging, comforting and urging you to live lives worthy of God, who calls you into his kingdom and glory. (1 Thessalonians 2:11–12)

A normal father simply doubles down on the stakes, pouring more of his time into his son's life and more of his heart into his son's soul. Had Jasen messed up, I'd have wrapped my arm around his shoulders and defended him, side by side. His failures could never make me love him less; they only make me yearn to love him better.

God is not only a normal Father but a perfect one, and there is only one way for His perfect heart to respond to your failure: love. Of course, you can *imagine* some other responses. You might think He's disgusted with you and would prefer if you got lost for a while. You can imagine that the sight of your face turns His stomach. You can even imagine that He's turned His back on you and—if not for His good character—would squash you like a bug.

But God can't imagine any of those things because He's your Father. It boils down to this: until you are free from prison, the full expression of His deep love for you isn't complete. He won't leave you, and nothing on earth—including your sexual sin and disobedience—can kill your Father's love.

If there's anyone who knows that, it's me. When my son Michael (now fourteen) joined the family, he was a terror. He couldn't sit still. He had to be climbing or running or tearing up the toy closet. He'd get into the cupboards and take out every board game and dump all their contents into one big pile. He'd go into the kitchen and take out every pot and pan and flip them onto the floor. When we were invited to the home of some respected church members for the first—and last—time, he jumped up on a coffee table, turned his rear toward the hostess, passed gas, then jumped down and ran away giggling. That same evening he threw a two-liter bottle of Sunkist Orange onto a tile floor, where it promptly began spinning and spraying a sticky mist in all directions. He laughed and danced in circles around it.

We reprimanded him, of course, but those early days were rugged. Michael stopped being invited to kiddy birthday parties, and our family stopped receiving dinner and barbecue invitations. Friends mocked my parenting skills right to my face.

Did I turn from Michael? No. I stayed right with him. I worked with him. I disciplined him. Michael felt the sting of more than a few spankings, I can assure you.

But his dad had his back. Michael wasn't what he should be, but I knew who and what he could be.

Perhaps the whole church knows about your sexual sin. Maybe your father is a deacon or a pastor, and people are mocking both of you behind your backs. But God stays right with you. He knows His dreams for you. He knows your potential. Can He bless you the way He'd like to? Not yet. Can you have the same intimacy with Him? Not yet. He's busy getting you back to normal, doing whatever it takes.

But His heart beats the same for you as it does for the obedient one. He has your back, and He's chasing your potential with all of His heart. His eyes are always on you.

My passion for Michael was never less than my passion for Jasen, just as God's passion for you will never be less than it is for anyone else. I couldn't turn my back on Michael, because he's a Stoeker and my boy. God can't turn His back on you, because you bear Christ's name and are His boy. Don't ever forget that.

Speaking with Power and Grace

Many believe that God is always hungry to harshly judge us for our sin, probably because we are so quick on that trigger ourselves. *Punish the insolent, and death to the infidels!*

I'm not at all immune to this attitude. By the time a pastor was called out for a sexual dalliance with a girl in our youth group, I'd just about had it with pastors and their sexual sin. Because of my connections to my denomination's state office, I was aware of similar problems all across Iowa. I was angry and frustrated because kids kept getting hurt by these pastors' failures.

But satisfaction was in sight. As providence would have it, I was asked to challenge a large group of pastors to deeper sexual purity at our denomination's annual meeting. I couldn't wait for that moment. Deep down, I wanted to give them a good tongue-lashing.

About an hour before I was to speak, Brenda and I knelt together in the prayer chapel in final preparation for my verbal shelling. Soon, however, the conviction of the Holy Spirit settled over me, and I was no longer sure that I had the right attitude. So I prayed, "Lord, I want Your heart as I speak to these men today. If the statistics are right, as many as half of these guys have been checking out porn this month, and You know how that frustrates me. After all, they are supposed to be our shepherds!

"But, Lord, I also know how You love Your cherished pastors. So I don't want to speak out of *my* feelings today. I want to speak out of Your feelings for them. Can You help me? Can You let me feel *Your* feelings toward Your pastors today?"

Instantly the Lord answered. Without warning, an overwhelming flood of desperate emotion pressed into my chest. It literally felt as though my heart would explode. Falling onto my side in deep, wrenching sobs, I found I could hardly breathe. About three minutes later, the waves of emotion and my feelings of panic stopped as quickly as they'd begun. The Lord whispered into my spirit, *There. Now you know how I ache for My cherished pastors, in spite of their sin. Speak to them from that aching place in My heart.*

Brenda later wrote in her journal, "Moments later Fred walked out and spoke with a grace and power I had never seen in him before."

God is not like us. God is love. That doesn't mean He'll never judge you or rebuke you for your sexual sin. He will at times. But that is only a sign of His total and complete love for you. You are a son, and a rebuke only goes to prove it:

In your struggle against sin, you have not yet resisted to the point of shedding your blood. And you have forgotten that word of encouragement that addresses you as sons:

"My son, do not make light of the Lord's discipline,
    and do not lose heart when he rebukes you,
because the Lord disciplines those he loves,
    and he punishes everyone he accepts as a son."

Endure hardship as discipline; God is treating you as sons. For what son is not disciplined by his father? If you are not disciplined (and everyone undergoes discipline), then you are illegitimate children and not true sons.... Our fathers disciplined us for a little while as they thought best; but God disciplines us for our good, that we may share in his holiness. (Hebrews 12:4–8, 10)

Even in judgment, your Father's only motive is love. God hates sin because it binds you mercilessly and cuts off your connection with Him. But He doesn't hate you, and you are not sickening to Him.

This is how God sees you (illustrated by some excerpts from e-mails I've received).

He sees your wounds:

My nephew feels that no one loves him, because his mom and father are completely uninvolved in his life. He keeps a *Sports Illustrated* swimsuit edition in his bathroom and masturbates when he's stressed out.

He sees your loneliness:

I just got out of a sexual relationship with a girl in my church that ruined our friendship, and now she isn't talking to me. The loneliness is almost unbearable. I know I can beat that sumo wrestler when he attacks with those sexual thoughts, but as soon as he gets tired of wrestling, he just tags out and his partner, Mr. Loneliness, steps into the ring and knocks me flat.

He sees your desperation:

I've been addicted to porn and masturbation for more than ten years. I've read books, done online courses, and had accountability partners, but it's still too easy to walk into a store and stare at lurid magazines. I turn to porn because I don't have much hope that I'll ever get married. Everyone at school used to laugh at me and tell me how ugly I was.

He sees you and everything about you, but now *you* have to see Him and His ways. You've got to understand *His* desperation to restore you if you are to ever understand His heart as He calls you to purity.

God is like the father who sidled up to the television where his co-workers were watching the Weather Channel and turned white in horror as live cameras caught a massive funnel cloud dipping and ripping into his neighborhood. A silent scream ripped through his heart. *My son is home alone! I've got to get to him!*

Sweat poured as his grip on the steering wheel turned his knuckles white. It took forty-five minutes to travel what would normally take ten minutes because the tornado had ripped down trees and power lines. Once he reached his neighborhood, though, a police roadblock wouldn't let him in, even though he pleaded with the officers, telling them that his boy was home alone—or maybe dead.

Making a U-turn, he squealed into the parking lot of a nearby golf course. After leaping out of the car, he raced across the fairways and sneaked into his neighborhood, running toward his house with all of his heart. In horror, he noticed that one neighbor's house had been flattened. The rumpled remains of a brand-new Ford Mustang stuck out of the front door of another.

When he reached his house, he stopped cold. The whole front of the house had been torn off, exposing the kitchen, family room, and upstairs bedrooms. The scene of devastation looked like a giant dollhouse at the department store.

"Ricky! Ricky!" he screamed.

As he ran into the obliterated house, he saw hundreds of glass shards sprayed across the walls. Terrified, he screamed even louder, "Ricky! Ricky!"

Suddenly he heard a faint voice from the basement, "Dad?" Clambering down through the rubble, he found his boy shaking, hiding in a bathtub.

Grabbing his son in his arms, he just stood there, hugging the boy. They bawled and bawled in relief and joy.

You've been caught up in a tornado of sexual activity. Your Father is racing to find you in the rubble and to put His arms around you. He's eager to forget how you offended Him or made bad choices. What He's after is your heart and your relationship, and He won't stop digging until He finds you.

For Personal Reflection

1. Was God's law given primarily for His benefit or our benefit?

2. How *must* a normal father's heart respond to his son's defeat? Why *must* he stay at your side until you are free?

3. If you are still losing, why can't God's passion for you be less than His passion for your more obedient brother?

11

A Father's Dreams

Your Father's heart beats endlessly after yours, but His unfailing love may leave you with too little urgency to line up with His Word. Yes, it's true; He won't leave you or ever stop loving you, regardless of your sexual—or other—sins.

However, don't ever forget the flip side to this truth: while His love is not affected by your disobedience, His dreams for you will always be connected to the level of your obedience.

Every father wants to help his son make something of himself. As Jasen exited his toddler years, I longed to teach him everything I knew. I sweated through my clothes when I taught him to ride his bike and labored over his swimming strokes. I threw passes, pitched batting practice, and shot baskets with him. I taught him how to win with grace and lose with honor. We read books together, and I prayed and worshiped at his side, providing for his spiritual growth and insight. God is no different from every other father. Your Father yearns to give you a head start in His kingdom and to send you out fully equipped to make your mark for Him:

> Have mercy on me, O God,
>   according to your unfailing love;

according to your great compassion
>   blot out my transgressions....

Restore to me the joy of your salvation
>   and grant me a willing spirit, to sustain me.

Then I will teach transgressors your ways,
>   and sinners will turn back to you. (Psalm 51:1, 12–13)

He did that in my life. He set me free from sexual sin and nudged me to write *Every Man's Battle* to give men some practical steps in their battles for purity. Then He freed *more* sons and sent them out to teach others, fully equipped to make their mark for Him.

Being of One Heart

Equipping you is only the start of your Father's dream for you. It's true that He wants you to make your mark in life, but what He really wants is for His boy to be just like Him. He wants to create something special with you—and help you find that place where your destiny intertwines completely with His. *That's* what means the world to Him, and that's where the true magic of the relationship lies. Today, you're His son. But someday, you'll both be of one heart, like brothers. He yearns to show you what the two of you can become together. That's His dream for you, and it's for the sake of His dreams that we must all remain urgent about obedience.

Naturally, He'll forgive you whenever you miss His mark, and, yes, it's true that His love for you won't change if you stumble and fall. This is the age of grace, after all.

But that doesn't make this the age of racing around and letting your eyes and heart take you wherever you want to go. Stopping short of His standards will stop you short of His dreams for you, and His grace can't do anything about that. To understand why, it might help to look at an earthly father's dream for his son.

My dream for Jasen was enormous, and I could only dream such a dream because the destinies of every father and son are forever intertwined. You see, Jasen has never been *just* my son, and he will never be *just* an individual—he's also a link in a very important chain.

My father was the last male in our family tree who bore the Stoeker name. My mother delivered just one son—that would be me—and I helped forge the next link in that chain through Jasen's birth. Will my son bear my name well? That question is central to every father's destiny. Jasen's position as a link to the next generation is crucial to my dreams, just as your spot in God's chain is critical to His dreams in heaven.

Now, I don't want you to mistake what I am saying here. God *is* very interested in you as an individual. Through Jesus, God came for you as an individual, and Jesus died for you as an individual. But He is also interested in you as a link in His family chain. He knows how easily the message of salvation is passed to the next generation of His children—new believers—when you are walking obediently in Christ, and that's why your obedience as a link in His family chain is so critical to your Father. He wants the family heritage to pass down easily and His family to flourish.

Every father wants that, and as for Jasen's spot in *my* chain, God wasted no time explaining these same principles to me through a tiny pair of scriptures He showed me a few months after my son was born. The first one involved a relatively obscure man in the Bible, a fellow named Jehonadab. But to find Jehonadab, we must look at the story of Jehu (see 2 Kings 10:15).

Now Jehu was one intense guy. Having received an order from God's prophet to overthrow wicked King Ahab, he had Ahab's seventy sons slaughtered and their heads heaped into two piles by Jezreel's city gate. The next morning Jehu arose with the sun and spent the morning killing everyone left in the city who remained loyal to the house of Ahab, including his chief men, his close friends, and his priests.

With no survivors left to kill, Jehu bolted Jezreel and tore down the road toward Samaria, where he intended to destroy every sign of Baal worship and kill every friend of Ahab he could find. Along the way Jehu spotted Jehonadab, son of Recab, which gave him a perfect chance to show off his zeal for God. Jehu quickly offered Jehonadab a ride so he could observe this reign of destruction from the back of his chariot, which was sort of like inviting Billy Graham along for the ride, since Jehonadab was known as one of the godliest men of his day. Jehonadab had constantly railed against Baal worship and called the people to worship the only true God.

After this little story in 2 Kings 10, we don't hear about Jehonadab again until the book of Jeremiah, where his name is spelled "Jonadab." At that time, God's people had been straying again and were totally ignoring Him, so God sent Jeremiah to visit Jehonadab's descendants. Here's what happened:

> This is the word that came to Jeremiah from the LORD...: "Go to the Recabite family and invite them to come to one of the side rooms of the house of the LORD and give them wine to drink."
>
> So I went to get...all his sons—the whole family of the Recabites. I brought them into the house of the LORD.... Then I set bowls full of wine and some cups before the men of the Recabite family and said to them, "Drink some wine."
>
> But they replied, "We do not drink wine, because our forefather Jonadab son of Recab gave us this command: 'Neither you nor your descendants must ever drink wine.'... We have obeyed everything our forefather Jonadab son of Recab commanded us." (Jeremiah 35:1–6, 8)

With God's help, Jeremiah caught the message loud and clear, which allowed him to speak an important truth against the children of Israel for the Lord's sake:

> Then the word of the LORD came to Jeremiah, saying: "This is what the LORD Almighty, the God of Israel, says: Go and tell the men of

Judah and the people of Jerusalem, 'Will you not learn a lesson and
obey my words?' declares the LORD. 'Jonadab son of Recab ordered his
sons not to drink wine and this command has been kept. To this day
they do not drink wine, because they obey their forefather's command.
But I have spoken to you again and again, yet you have not obeyed
me.'" (Jeremiah 35:12–14)

While the term *sons* meant "descendants," it probably included disciples
as well. In any event, what's interesting is that more than two hundred years
had passed since Jehonadab set his example for these descendants. *Two hundred years!* The purifying work he began in his family tree was still being felt
at least ten generations later.

As I pondered Jehonadab's impact upon his family, I wondered if I could
purify my branch of the family tree by declaring before God that I would
make every effort to cause *my* family to follow Him in their sexuality. Perhaps
my part of the family tree would flourish as I pruned it with godly behavior.
Perhaps folks two hundred years from now would remember that once my
branch on the tree sprouted, generations were influenced for good.

As I meditated further, I considered how much Jehonadab reminded me
of the great-great-grandmother of my pastor, John Palmer. This woman turned
to Christ in the late 1800s from a godless background. Her Christian example
was so powerful that every descendant over the next hundred years has been
either a pastor, a pastor's wife, a missionary, or a missionary's wife, at least until
just recently. That's one solid limb in the family tree.

By contrast, my family tree teemed with sin. In its branches were adultery,
pornography, incest, sexual abuse, physical abuse, and many examples of hatred,
discord, jealousy, fits of rage, selfish ambition, carousing, drunkenness, and the
like. I knew some of those characteristics were ingrained in me as well, which
would make my new quest that much tougher. I wanted to prune away the
dead section of my family tree and grow a new branch that would be strong
in Christ.

There were, however, two problems with this plan. First of all, I wasn't too sure it was even possible. Perhaps Jehonadab wondered the same thing. In his day you drank water, milk, or wine; there wasn't much else. For someone like Jehonadab to cut wine out of his life must have seemed rather odd, and yet generations of Jehonadab's descendants did exactly that for more than two hundred years.

Today, many guys believe it's rather odd to consider cutting sensuality out of their lives. They believe that masturbation is inevitable. But after reading Jehonadab's story, I couldn't help thinking that if he could do the impossible in regard to wine, perhaps I could do the impossible in regard to sensuality.

The Next Link in the Chain

The biggest hurdle looming for me as a father was that, unlike my individual battle for purity, I couldn't accomplish this call on my own. Eventually someone else in the chain would have to buy into my vision and would have to trust my love enough to bravely make the same decision. That someone would have to be a real man and a son—in this case, Jasen. He is my spiritual heir, the next link in my chain. He would be the very key to God's call and vision for my life as a father.

Jasen had to become that real man I needed at my side, or I'd fail. How does a boy become such a man? In our world, sex is a guy's rite of passage into manhood. You simply aren't a man until you've done it with a girl. But the rite of passage in God's world is entirely different; doing it with a girl outside of marriage only proves you've chosen the ways of the world instead of the ways of God.

So what should be your rite of passage into manhood? Let's take a look at what Jesus considered to be such a normal rite.

When He was twelve years old and traveled with his parents to Jerusalem, He got so caught up in some discussions with the religious scholars at the temple that He stayed behind when His parents left for home. When His mother finally found Him and asked what He was doing, Jesus responded respectfully, "Why did you seek Me? Did you not know that I must be about My Father's business?" (Luke 2:49, NKJV).

Being about our father's business is our true rite of passage into manhood. Jesus was about His Father's business from the start, which shouldn't surprise us, because He had a transformed mind from the start. Jesus was always in line with His Father's vision:

I do nothing on my own but speak just what the Father has taught me. (John 8:28)

[The Son] can do only what he sees his Father doing, because whatever the Father does the Son also does. (John 5:19)

You are God's son. Complete obedience is a normal part of being about your Father's business in His kingdom, and if your earthly dad's dreams are aligned with God's purposes for your family, being about your earthly father's business will be just as normal as well.

Consider Jasen's position. I had chosen to start a new branch on the family tree that reflected the mind of Christ. When Jasen was about twelve (about the same age Jesus was during His trip to Jerusalem), Jasen heard me explain how I had turned my back on sexual sin for the sake of my relationship with God—and for Jasen's future—and how this was part of God's vision for our family. As Jesus did at that age, Jasen somehow knew it was time to be about my business—and God's business—with all of his heart. He caught God's vision for us as father and son. That was his rite of passage into manhood, and with that decision he became that real man I needed at my side to complete our destinies in God together.

Jasen never chafed or asked, "How far can I go sexually and still get by with Dad?" Such questions made no sense in the context of the linked relationship between a father and son; his disobedience would always affect my family dream. He knew we were one in this call, and he was willing to pay the price of shouldering this business with me.

It's a good thing too, because the sacrifices started early. One day in seventh grade, Jasen's teacher pulled out a PG-rated film to show the class as a reward for a couple of weeks of hard work. Jasen knew what PG stood for—"Parental Guidance"—and that was good enough for him. Since he hadn't been able to ask us ahead of time if the film was okay to watch, he simply walked up to the teacher and asked if he could sit this one out in the hallway. The kids chuckled at him on his way out, but he trusted his mom and me.

Because school can be such an awful place, another time Jasen arrived home hurting. "Mom, I had an awful day in school," he said to Brenda. "This morning just after the bell, Jayla stood up in front of the whole room and said, 'Hey, class, I have a question for all of us. Since Jasen just turned fourteen, how come he's not allowed to go to PG-13 movies?' "

"Jayla said that? That's awful!" Brenda exclaimed. "What happened next?"

"Mom, I wanted to die. Everything went quiet, and everyone stared at me."

"What did the teacher do?"

"She about tore Jayla's head off, but I still felt so small, Mom. I wondered if I'd ever have any friends again."

Obedience is costly, and no father asks for his son's obedience lightly. Suffering heavy social costs can lead a son to question, *If God loves me, should I really have to suffer like this?*

I suffer like crazy when my kids are pushed away or laughed at as losers, and it kills me when even church kids mock them, saying, "It's Christians like you that give Christianity a bad name."

I've been surprised at the relentless pounding my kids have taken at church, and I have to admit that I've second-guessed myself as a father on a few occasions: *Have I been cruel to ask my children to join me in this family quest? Could I have missed something? Perhaps God doesn't expect us to walk this purely after all.*

Every father hates to see his son suffer, and your heavenly Father is no different. He aches when you suffer for Him. But this Father is also different from other fathers: He is never surprised by anything and never second-guesses what He believes. What's more, He's known forever what I'm only beginning to learn: social suffering makes a man strong. You should rejoice in it, because in the end, suffering builds great hope in your heart, just as the Bible says:

Not only so, but we also rejoice in our sufferings, because we know
that suffering produces perseverance; perseverance, character; and character, hope. And hope does not disappoint us, because God has poured
out his love into our hearts by the Holy Spirit, whom he has given us.
(Romans 5:3–5)

You can expect social suffering as you walk purely like your Father. That's
a normal part of your destiny. Jasen has suffered the slings and arrows, but I
know a work is being finished in my son:

You know that the testing of your faith develops perseverance. Perseverance must finish its work so that you may be mature and complete, not
lacking anything. (James 1:3–4)

Jasen's sexual freedom is complete, and he has thanked me countless times
for this freedom. He has also matured and lacks nothing, just as God's Word
promises, and he's a real man to be reckoned with on purity's battlefield.

I was reminded of this the last time we watched *Star Trek: The Next Generation* on video. Midway through the show, First Officer Will Riker and
Counselor Deanna Troi suddenly appeared on the screen, sitting on opposite
sides of a deep hot tub with soap bubbles covering everything up to their
necks. The scene did not turn sensual, but Jasen quietly exited the living room
immediately because he didn't want to expose himself *if* things heated up between Riker and Troi.

Now that's obedience.

Staying the Course

Though Jasen's out of the home and on his way in life, my heart bubbles over
whenever I think about him. He has sacrificed at my side for our destiny and
for our name, and his normal, faithful obedience has fulfilled my dreams for

him and for us. Jasen's life is my proof that we've accomplished something spe-cial together, as the following story illustrates.

As a Campus Crusade leader, Jasen recently told me that a couple of guys asked him if he'd use my book *Every Man's Challenge* in their small-group book study at Iowa State University. When he mentioned this, I said, "Jace, you know how careful I've been about your purity through the years, and you know that some of the topics I write on are a bit graphic. Before I give you the book to read, is there any topic you might like me to censor?"

"I don't want to read anything about masturbation," he replied simply. "I don't know much about it, and I don't want to know any more." I knew why he said that: he didn't want to get caught up in all the talk about masturbation because of where it could lead and how it could impact his purity.

But what an unbelievable statement for any young man to make in this day and age! Keep in mind that Jasen is twenty-two years old, and our sex-on-the-brain culture has swirled around him freely for years. He was raised in a public school system and has attended a major state university for the past four years. He is a gifted computer engineer and could probably skirt his way around any antiporn software on the planet. He's had every opportunity to go a different way in life.

But he hasn't, and now our destinies have been fulfilled together. My old-est son is just like me, and we've created a brand-new branch in our family tree. And yet Jasen has become more than my son; he is also my brother in Christ.

This is what your obedience will mean to your Father in heaven. Like Jasen's obedience in my family, your obedience is your heavenly Father's hope for seeing His dreams accomplished in His family and in the lost hearts around you. Sure, there is a cost to step up to the plate. But if you stay in the box and don't flinch when the high, inside fastballs come your way, blessing after blessing will pour out of His marveling heart and into your life. He won't be able to help Himself because of His overwhelming delight in you. You will have become one in heart, a brother of Christ in the same family:

Both the one who makes men holy and those who are made holy are
of the same family. So Jesus is not ashamed to call them brothers.
(Hebrews 2:11)

God wants His boy—you—to be just like Him. No matter what the suffering, no matter what the cost, this is what your Father calls you to deliver to
the family of God. He wants His family to be normal and flourishing. He
knows that as His sons pick up on His dream and vision for His family chain
and kingdom, the godly pattern that results will draw all men to Christ.

Once you fully buy into God's dreams for you as His son, His trust ramps
up as you take your place as Christ's brother and warrior in His kingdom.

In the next chapter, we'll see how this unfolds in practice as you begin to
bless your Father's heart.

For Personal Reflection

1. If God's love won't be killed by your sin, why is it still important to
   remain urgent about your obedience?
2. What does God need from you in order to accomplish His dreams
   for your branch of His family tree?
3. A non-Christian's rite of passage into manhood might be sex. As a
   Christian, what is your rite of passage into manhood?
4. What does God call you—and for that matter, every man—to
   deliver to the family of God?

12

A Father's Trust

And we, who with unveiled faces all reflect the Lord's glory,
are being transformed into his likeness
with ever-increasing glory, which comes from the Lord,
who is the Spirit.

—2 CORINTHIANS 3:18

In *Every Man's Battle* I described three defensive perimeters that you have to erect before you can experience total freedom from sexual sin:

1. Bounce the eyes.
2. Starve your mind.
3. Cherish your wife.

If my correspondence is any indication, bouncing the eyes seems to capture the most attention from my readers, and this doesn't surprise me. A guy spends his years spinning in circles and bound by dark sexual chains while the Enemy mocks him endlessly, whispering, *God's promises will never work for you!* Suddenly *Every Man's Battle* suggests a practical solution like bouncing the eyes, and the light dawns for him. Joe Regular can get his head around *that* concept, so he grabs at it like a paratrooper snatching his rip cord.

Besides, bouncing the eyes works big time. The simple act of turning your gaze away from a sexual image—a girl's breasts or her navel—isn't easy to do when you're used to viewing eye candy, but doing so breaks the addictive chemical cycle that's choking you.

Averting your vision is the right thing to do. After all, you're called to *conform* and *act* like Jesus, and without a doubt that's the key to every man's jail cell. But if you're to keep that jailhouse a distant memory, you must be *transformed* by the Word to *think* like Jesus. The following verse explains this well:

> Do not be conformed to this world (this age), [fashioned after and
> adapted to its external, superficial customs], but be transformed
> (changed) by the [entire] renewal of your mind [by its new ideals
> and its new attitude]. (Romans 12:2, AMP)

Jesus gave up His rights and became a servant so that He could buy us back at a price. From then on, His Master in heaven held all the rights to His life. Jesus was no longer His own.

Once Jesus paid that steep price for you at Calvary, you are no longer your own, either. You have no right to think about life and relationships in any way but His way. The following verse is the foundation of the transformed, servant mind-set like the one Jesus had:

> Flee from sexual immorality.... You are not your own; you were bought
> at a price. Therefore honor God with your body. (1 Corinthians
> 6:18–20)

It's also the foundation for your total victory over sexual sin. During my battle for sexual purity, I distilled this essential scripture down to its core, which eventually worked to transform my mind completely: *You have no right to look at that or think about it. You haven't the authority.*

The power of temptation wanes quickly in your life once your mind is transformed to think this way. That is because Satan's capacity to tempt you lies in your mind-set; if you believe you have no right to choose what you want to look at, no temptation in the world can lay a glove on you.

When your buddy e-mails his sizzling porn queen and begs you to check out the hottest PDF attachment you've ever seen, you simply delete the message without a thought. It's an instant reaction: *I simply have no right to look.* There are no questions like "Should I?" or "Shouldn't I?" You are His, and you're fine with that.

If you *aren't* transformed, of course, you're still wide open to discuss the pros and cons with yourself, and if that's the case, you might as well ask Satan to join the discussion. Believe me, he would *love* to be heard on this issue. Given half a chance, the Enemy pours a flood of compelling reasons through your brain, and you're so focused upon his arguments that you don't notice the flames of lust rising higher and licking at your senses until it's too late. By that time, your body's on fire, and when that happens, you'll readily accept any grounds he's provided for giving in "just this once" and clicking on the alluring attachment. That's where the power of temptation lies.

If you're a servant with a transformed mind, though, you're not asking yourself rhetorical questions like "Should I?" or "Shouldn't I?" Your answer was "No" long before Satan got to your door. It is only in this final transformation that freedom from sexual sin can reign completely. You become a slave to righteousness rather than a slave to impurity. Once you've given up your right to choose your own way, you are truly crucified in Christ. The old you is dead, and your decisions are being made beyond the letter of the law and even beyond the range of Satan's voice.

Something deep and profound has happened. You no longer chafe at God's standards because your attitude is, *I haven't a right.* That truth is so ingrained and your mind is so transformed that the right "choice" is made even before the sexual issue arises.

Walking the straight and narrow is easy. It's the only path you have the right to use. You're His servant, and everything is settled. Obedience is automatic. There isn't an issue more vital for total victory over sexual sin than the issue of rights, because this is where the death of sexual temptation becomes imminent.

Some believe that temptation will always be there, like a parrot sitting on your shoulder, chirping away. They cite Paul's struggles with temptation, pointing out that he sometimes felt compelled to do some things he didn't want to do because of his flesh (see Romans 7:14–25).

I will concede that point, of course, because it explains why we will never be sinless while living upon this earth. I also agree that Satan will never stop firing his grenades of temptation at us. You can count on it: the prince of darkness will never quit lurking around your backyard.

But that's as far as I can agree to go, because I also know we have Christ's power and grace working on our behalf. I believe that the power of Satan's temptation will diminish and that obedience can be automatic. We *can* climb to a point where fewer temptations can be lobbed our way. I know it because I've lived there.

Paul had to know this too. After all, this was the same Paul who claimed it was for freedom that Christ set us free, not for more bondage (Galatians 5:1). He declared that we could live a brand-new life down here because of Christ's resurrection, not the same old mediocre one (see Romans 6:4). Once you say that the power of Satan's temptations will never subside, you're also saying that the new life Christ placed in you is perpetually powerless to change anything for you here on earth. I don't see things that way.

I've found that God is strong in ways that I never could have imagined, and He wants you strong as well. He wants to teach you to find those ways of escape more easily, which He alluded to in this scripture:

But when you are tempted, he will also provide a way out so that you
can stand up under it. (1 Corinthians 10:13)

He wants you to be transformed into the image of Christ, moving from glory to glory (see 2 Corinthians 3:18, NASB), so that you can do even greater exploits than He did (see John 14:12). That just isn't possible if the power of temptation never weakens and our discernment of Satan's lies never sharpens.

Think about it: our Lord loved us enough to be crucified and sanctified on our behalf (see John 17:19, AMP). Would He do everything that He did for us at Calvary only to leave us struggling hopelessly against temptation for the rest of our lives? No way, as this scripture confirms:

> If God didn't hesitate to put everything on the line for us, embracing
> our condition and exposing himself to the worst by sending his own
> Son, is there anything else he wouldn't gladly and freely do for us?
> (Romans 8:32, MSG)

Your heavenly Father wants you to walk normally, like Jesus. If Paul actually meant that you can never really walk normally again in the face of temptation, what good is Christianity? And what good would the rest of the Bible be to us? The contradictions would be endless, and the apostle Paul would be left with no choice but to call the apostle Peter a bold-faced liar for telling us that we have been given everything we need to take part in the divine nature (see 2 Peter 1:3–4).

But God has good news for you. The truth is, your mind *can* be transformed enough to resist temptation:

> Don't become so well-adjusted to your culture that you fit into it with-
> out even thinking. Instead, fix your attention on God. You'll be
> changed from the inside out. Readily recognize what he wants from
> you, and quickly respond to it. Unlike the culture around you, always
> dragging you down to its level of immaturity, God brings the best out
> of you, develops well-formed maturity in you. (Romans 12:2, MSG)

That's especially good news, because if the power of temptation never fades, how would God ever be able to trust you in ministry, for example? When I founded an intercession prayer group at my church and watched it grow in numbers and strength, I often felt amazed—and sometimes overwhelmed. I once prayed in frustration, "Lord, why in the world did You choose me for

this important position? I seem to have no gifts for it, and I don't feel quali-
fied at all!"

His answer jolted me: *If you hadn't taken care of your sexual sin, I could not
have used you in this way. I wouldn't have been able to trust you with the women.*

I was left spellbound by His answer, although it immediately made sense.
First of all, these groups are filled mostly with women. Second, intercession is
intensely intimate. People pour out their most painful emotions and deepest
spiritual longings in complete trust and openness time after time, week after
week. This intense interpersonal intimacy flows so freely that the group can
easily become fertile ground for adulterous eyes and wavering hearts.

That's why I knew instantly what the Lord meant when He told me that
He couldn't have used me as an intercession leader if I hadn't taken care of my
sexual sin long ago. He didn't choose me to lead because I was gifted spiritually. He chose me because He could trust me.

Don't Miss Your Destiny

You may not be taking your walk with the Lord seriously enough for Him to
trust you with important work. You need to get serious now if you expect an
important destiny to unfold with Him later on.

Consider this: I engaged my battle for purity more than ten years before
the Lord would need someone to lead that prayer group. At one time, I would
have laughed in your face had you told me that I would one day lead a prayer
group. I can assure you that when I was engaged in the battle for purity, I had
no idea that God had a great prayer destiny planned for me. And, as it turns
out, I would have missed my destiny had I not been faithful years earlier to
what the Bible asked me to do. I'm glad I chose complete obedience from the
get-go. When God's eyes were going to and fro, looking for someone to lead
our intercession group, His eyes stopped on me, and it wasn't because I was
special or gifted. It was because I was ready.

Have you allowed His transforming work to have its way with you? Is sexual obedience becoming automatic, and is the power of temptation fading in your life?

God is searching for trustworthy sons to call into great service, but you can't expect that call if your behavior has been untrustworthy. God is also looking for the guy who will offer Him up front everything he has, even before he knows what God has planned for him.

If you're living in spiritual mediocrity while waiting for the Lord to ask you to join with Him in His kingdom work, you have a long wait ahead. Meanwhile, you go about your lukewarm life tickling your sexuality with Hollywood films, questionable concerts, and weak-willed women, wondering why it's taking so long for Him to bang on your door. As long as He's taking His sweet time about it, you're happy to keep from becoming "too Christian" before you absolutely have to. Check out what this mother wrote:

> My son is dating our pastor's daughter, and one recent Saturday morning he told me he'd purchased a couple of tickets to a punk-rap concert in Portland. I have to admit I was shocked, because I'd stumbled across a newspaper article about these rappers a few weeks earlier, so I knew their lyrics were outlandishly sensual and violent. When his girlfriend joined us for dinner that night, I casually mentioned what I'd read in the newspaper about these rappers. With a perky grin and a light toss of her head, my son's girlfriend said brightly, "Well, we should never get too Christian to have any fun!"

When I read e-mails like these, I'm glad I got in line with the Lord early so that He could plan bigger dreams for me. I also can't help remembering what my wife, Brenda, wrote about me in *Every Heart Restored:*

> I feel incredible security knowing that I'm married to a man who keeps his eyes to himself. Even after four babies and twenty-four years of aging together, I live unthreatened by any women around me. Fred

loves me for me and is very satisfied with who I am and what I've become.

When my husband prays, I'm confident that nothing is hindering his connection with God. If I knew of dark, hidden areas, I'd have no faith that his prayers would even rise to the ceiling, but I've seen how a pure man's prayer packs a spiritual punch.

My confidence in Fred's spiritual protection is unbounded. I never wonder if there are open cracks in our spiritual defenses where the Enemy can slip into our lives. Christianity is not a game to Fred, and image means nothing. He'd rather *be* a Christian than seem like one.

Fred has every right to make the decisions for our family because it's God's plan, but even if it weren't, he's earned that right through his actions. He's proven in battle that his commitment to the Lord and his love for his family are the highest priorities in his life, and we simply rest in his strength.

This normal, godly pattern leaves everyone flourishing, and this wouldn't be possible if blatant sin were clogging things up. I know who Fred is, and in the secret places of life, I know where he will not go.

This kind of trust will be vital in your marriage one day, but it is even more vital in your relationship with Christ right now. If the Lord plans on giving you great work to do, He'll need to trust you. He needs to see you're trustworthy in the secret places of your life. After all, He loves you. He doesn't want you to get in over your head spiritually so that you might bring shame on the name of Christ and your friends and family.

There can be no oneness and tight intimacy with the Lord without trust. Trust is the basis of all relationships, but trust is a funny thing. It can't exist in a vacuum. No matter how desperately you want it, you can't manufacture trust on your own. If trust is expected to grow, each individual in a relationship is responsible for bringing the main ingredient—trustworthiness—to the table.

Love and commitment are entirely different from trust. God's love for you can exist in a vacuum, because He can choose to love you no matter how you act. It's the same way with God's commitment. He committed His heart to saving you before you even had a relationship with Him.

But trust can't exist on its own like this. Trust can only exist in relationship, and real trust can only come when the Father has full confidence in your faithfulness. Only one thing can bring that confidence to the Lord: your consistent, faithful action. Winning His trust requires plenty from you, like an immense change of character and the complete obedience of a transformed mind.

There's no trick to gaining God's trust. You earn it by taking on the mind of Christ as you go through life, showing your Father that He can count on you to make the right choices, whether you're sitting alone with a pretty girl or sitting alone with your computer in your dorm room.

You may not like taking on the mind of Christ because that might short-circuit your fun. But you'll never develop any trust between you and your heavenly Father until you do. As long as you are double-minded about your commitment to His ways, He can't trust you with a great work and destiny—to be His man and His warrior.

If you don't feel much like a warrior at the moment, remember this: God knows exactly who you are. God's known what you are made of since the dawn of time—dust. But He also knows that He's deposited a new life in you and sent the Comforter to walk at your side, so your immunity to temptation will rocket higher as you abide in Him. You *will* become a warrior, living freely in Him. You don't have to remain the Enemy's victim.

Still Looking to Nail You

Satan does not give up easily, of course. Once he aimed a cruise missile my way and tried to destroy everything I'd worked for. It happened on the very night I signed the contract to publish *Every Man's Battle*. Inking that contract was the biggest moment of my Christian life. I'd invested more than two years in getting the important message of that book on paper, a message that told the whole world about my Father's great work in my life.

That night I fell asleep at Brenda's side and innocently stumbled into an intense dream. I found myself sitting under the leafy canopy of a stout oak tree in the middle of a luscious green meadow. Then suddenly—plop—a nude, enticing woman was on my lap, gazing into my face with wanton eyes. I hadn't had a sensual dream about another woman in more than ten years, yet out of the blue, there she was without a stitch of clothing. Without even a hint of mental grappling, I simply set this beautiful woman on the ground, stood up, and calmly walked away. Dream over.

Satan had a lot of gall to try to get me to lust after another woman on the very day I signed the *Every Man's Battle* contract. He wanted to take me out by playing with my head and undermining my fitness to be a spokesman for this series. But the plan backfired, and all his little dream proved was that God's victory can sap the power of Satan's temptations in a man's life.

This wasn't the last time Satan tried to undercut me. Another time I flew into Little Rock, Arkansas, for my first national radio broadcast. I arrived at the hotel late in the afternoon on the day before they needed me, which left me with a whole evening on my own.

This may sound strange to you, but the instant I stepped into my hotel room, I felt an evil presence. It was as if I'd stepped into a Frank Peretti novel; Satan was in the house. My mind flashed back to past times on the road where I would stay in hotel rooms and fight off sexual temptations deep into the night. On this occasion in Little Rock, I knew why the Enemy was paying a social call: he wanted to engage me in another one of those exhausting, faith-sapping fights that would ruin my courage for the next morning's broadcast.

This time things were different because I'd been transformed. I addressed Satan head-on with disdainful laughter. "Oh, really now!" I blurted out loud. "I should have known you'd try something like this!" Then, with a fierce fire that burned from my belly, I snarled, "Get out of here right now, in the name of Jesus. I've had it with you, and I won't have this tonight!"

Poof! The Enemy's presence evaporated, and I didn't sense him again all night. I slept like a baby, and the broadcast taping went beautifully the next morning.

In another lonely hotel room in Alton, Illinois, I turned in early because I was to speak to forty pastors and their spouses the following day on the topic of sexual purity. Two hours into my night's sleep, I was awakened by sensual groaning and moaning from the next room. For more than an hour, I was treated to the passionate wailings of a woman's buildup to orgasm after orgasm. It was wall-pounding stuff. Eventually they wore each other out, and I fell asleep, only to be awakened at dawn by another round of their passions.

Wailing like that can get your motor running, and at one time I would have gone along for the ride in my fantasies and masturbated along with their "music." But on this occasion, I didn't waver. I simply clamped down on my thoughts and took every one of them captive, keeping everything in check.

I didn't awake particularly fresh that morning, but I *did* awake victorious, ready to minister to a fine group of pastors. Now when I hear some say that our tolerance level for temptation never changes, my rebuttal is that our tolerance level for temptation *does* change—and for the better.

Your Father intends a better kind of life for you too. When you seek God's face intently and chase His ways completely, you'll soon discover the limits of Satan's power. His temptations can and will fade in your life, and you are not helpless before his assaults. You can hold your own through God's grace and the working of the Holy Spirit in you. You can grow, and His power can flow.

So how exactly can a man like you chase after God for this kind of transformation of your mind? Let's find out in the following section.

For Personal Reflection

1. What is the difference between being *conformed* to Christ in your *actions* and being *transformed* by Christ in your *thinking*?
2. How does the transformed mind change your response to temptation?

3. Ponder these questions again from pages 148–49: Have you allowed God's transforming work to have its way with you? Is sexual obedience becoming automatic, and is the power of temptation fading in your life?

4. What does God know about where you will and won't go in the secret places of your life?

5. By its nature, how is trust completely different from love?

EXPERIENCING YOUR FATHER

Now that you've had a chance to know more about the Father's love and the kind of dreams He has for you, it's time to seek a relationship with all of your heart. He's told you that once you do, you will find Him:

You will seek me and find me when you seek me with all your heart. (Jeremiah 29:13)

Jesus has always had a close relationship with the Father. And we know that Adam walked side by side with God in the cool of the day, but many of us have nowhere near this kind of intimacy because we spend little time with the Lord—in His garden or anywhere else. Check out what these readers told me:

- I want to be a pastor, and I'm on the youth-group praise team, but I have so much sexual sin that I have been forsaking prayer and reading the Word. I sense little communion with the Holy Spirit. I'm miserable. What should I do?

- I don't feel like I have a very good relationship with the Lord. I try to pray sometimes, but I usually forget. I'm trying to listen to Christian music, and that helps. But I just feel like there's a wall between me and God and that I'm not experiencing Christ as I should.
- Today I had a realization that I really haven't even put up a fight yet. It's like I'm not even giving God a chance when I get my urges. All of my life I have given porn the first chance, and my life has been pretty miserable.

If you've been a Christian for any length of time, you've heard it said that you'll only be as close to God as you choose to be. How close have you chosen to be to Him so far?

As you've considered your Father's love for you and caught a glimpse of the endless joy of running that race of destiny with Him, perhaps you've decided it's time to go further. How do you go about that?

First of all, you must remember that you're never alone when you're seeking God's face:

The Friend, the Holy Spirit whom the Father will send at my request,
will make everything plain to you. He will remind you of all the things
I have told you. (John 14:26, MSG)

Your Friend has also been referred to as your Comforter, Counselor, Helper, Intercessor, and Advocate. I can assure you that He's continually drawn me toward a deeper love and passion for Jesus and my Father. That's the role He plays in your life too, and you can take it from me: He plays His role perfectly.

I have spent most of my time dwelling upon *your* responsibilities in the battle for purity in both *Every Young Man's Battle* and *Tactics,* and I did that on purpose, because God expects you to play your role well. Having said that, I must make one more thing crystal clear: without the Holy Spirit, you will be nothing but charred toast on the sexual battlefield. He's more than your good friend. He has real power and an unbelievable connection with you and your Father. Best of all, He doesn't lose and doesn't intend to let you lose, either.

The apostle Paul tells us in his New Testament letters that the Holy Spirit guides, challenges, warns, confirms, renews, and sanctifies. He even preaches and prays through you, generously distributing ministry gifts into your hands and pouring God's love all over you.

You need to open your heart completely to the work of the Holy Spirit. Sure, He's a bit mysterious. His work has appeared a bit frightening to me at times, even after living with Him for years. But as you open up your heart and He continues to fill you with His presence, you'll find that He's your best and truest friend on the planet, and He will kick down the prison walls and fearlessly charge into the teeth of enemy fire with you.

All God asks of you in return is to be wide open to the Holy Spirit. He's probably bigger and more creative than your finite mind has imagined Him to be, but that's good. Expect Him to stretch your understanding for the rest of your days, because you'll need all of the resources He can muster in your life. So if you want to experience God more deeply, you'll need to ask your Father to open your mind and heart to the Holy Spirit's work.

Now, while the apostle Paul extolled the Holy Spirit's power again and again in his writings, he *also* suggested there's a place for self-discipline in your race with destiny:

> Do you not know that in a race all the runners run, but only one gets the prize? Run in such a way as to get the prize.... *Therefore I do not run like a man running aimlessly; I do not fight like a man beating the air.* (1 Corinthians 9:24, 26)

In these postmodern days, the word *discipline* has somehow fallen out of favor with Christians. Guys more often say, "I don't want to get all bogged down by the daily rules and rituals of Bible study and prayer. I'd rather just *experience* God!"

I understand this sentiment perfectly, and every last one of us needs to desire such experience. But if you want Him to be so close that you can actually sense Him as your audience of One, you'll have to seek His face with all your heart. That's His way and always has been His way, so that means there's no way around it. Discipline will be part of your race, and you will have to spend regular time studying Him, listening to Him, and telling Him how much you care.

Your intimacy with the Father—loving Him with all of your heart, soul, and mind—will be critical in learning how to own the field. In fact, Jesus called it the greatest commandment we have. I like things simply stated, so here's a paraphrase that helps me grasp the meaning of the Great Commandment: *you should live your life for an audience of One.*

If you expect to live successfully for this audience of One, your intimacy with Him had better be as real as what you feel when you pull your girlfriend up tight for a kiss under the stars. Or at least pretty close.

Jamie has the right idea:

> I am a freshman at Southern Cal, and the temptations on campus are very great, but I am excited to begin my battle for sexual purity with the defenses you've laid out in *Every Young Man's Battle.* Still, I want you to know that this isn't going to be my sole focus. I feel like God is calling me into a closer relationship with Him, so I will also be focusing on that relationship instead of just focusing on my sin. God's love for us is truly amazing, and I am so glad that He chose me to be His child!

I'm confident that God is calling you into a closer relationship with Him too. We'll take a closer look at how you get there in this section.

Experiencing the Father in Prayer

I know why a lot of guys don't pray much: it feels like too much effort. You have to set such a clear-cut time to make it happen, and when you *do* close your eyes to communicate with God, it's tough to concentrate on the task at hand.

Praying when you're in the throes of sexual sin is doubly difficult, because guilt has built a wall between you and the Lord, stunting your spiritual growth.

I can say this with confidence because this is how I felt about prayer in the midst of my early ups and downs as a Christian. I remember playing philosopher and rationalizing the way things ought to be. For instance, I figured, *Why pray? What's the difference anyway? I'll probably blow it tomorrow, and besides, God's sovereign! He's going to do what He wants to do anyway, whether I pray or not.*

I dismissed the importance of prayer and salved my conscience by convincing myself that my best course of action was to forget about it. After all, it didn't seem to be costing me much to ignore it. My young business was growing rapidly, and my marriage was finally blossoming beyond my wildest dreams.

What I didn't notice at the time was that I was missing the point entirely.

Sure, I was able to manage a pretty decent life without prayer, but there was no way I could *experience* God without it. There was no way I'd ever find my destiny without it, either. All I was destined to do at that point was miss the best dreams He had planned for my life with him.

Going through life without prayer is like playing wide receiver and never joining the huddle. Your own prodigious talent may somehow allow you to play a decent game, but your Quarterback will never engage you as He could have.

You'll never truly become one with the Lord without prayer. So where does your prayer life rank on the scale of possibilities with Him? Respond yes or no to this pop quiz question:

Are your prayer times with the Lord so intimate that they rock your emotions as deeply as sex or masturbation?

If you answered no, your prayer life isn't all that it could be, my friend. You can and *should* go much deeper with Him. Take it from a guy who once wouldn't give prayer a chance: it is well worth the effort to get there.

What is prayer like once you begin to get the upper hand on your sexual impurity? Garrett answered a similar question in *Every Young Man's Battle* when he said, "I used to get lustful thoughts popping up all the time during prayer. But now that my eyes are protected, it doesn't happen, so prayer has become so much deeper and uninterrupted."

This was the first change that I noticed too. Once I rooted out the sexual sin in my life, I had a real focus and peace, and I found it much easier to gather my thoughts and contemplate the Lord during those quiet times with Him.

A Change in Attitude

As my prayer life improved, I also noticed a profound change in my attitude as I prayed. No longer did I feel too unworthy to be heard because of my sin. No longer did I whine in tears and discouragement, hoping that God might find it in His heart to listen to me if I could only make Him feel sorry enough for me. Now my attitude was, *I'm His son. I'm worthy to be heard. He'll listen to me because fathers listen to sons, no matter what they've done.*

You're more than worthy for God to listen to you. I was reminded of this when Jasen was thirteen and had labored through a hot, dismal football practice after an extremely long day of testing in school. I took him and the family to Pizza Hut to cheer him up, but a beastly bundle of homework awaited Jasen after dinner.

As I recall, he didn't say much as he munched on his Canadian-bacon-and-pineapple pizza, but after we drove home and headed into the house for the evening, Jasen finally buckled a bit. "Dad, I've had a rotten day," he said.

"What's the matter, Son?"

He glanced around to see if any of his siblings were listening. I could tell he wanted to talk alone. "Whaddya say we go up to your bedroom and talk about it there," I said as I led him into the house.

"Okay, Dad," he mumbled.

I followed him to his bedroom, where he flopped himself backward onto his bed in an odd, discouraged way. It hurt me to see him like that.

"Sit up, Son. You'll feel better, and besides, I need to hear you face to face." He did as I requested. "Now, tell me all about it."

Jason sighed and began to dump his feelings, but he spoke in such a mumbled sort of whine that I had trouble understanding him. I asked him several times to repeat himself, but it was no use. Finally I said, "Jasen. Stop. You are my son. I'm your dad. Just tell me in your normal voice so I can hear."

All I wanted to hear was his heart. He didn't have to mumble or whine to make me feel sorry for him. He didn't have to convince me that his situation was worthy of my time. I cared about it from the moment he brought it up, simply because he was my son. I love him, and that's enough to draw my heart and attention to him any time, day or night.

Your Father loves you too. He cares, and He longs to hear from you. Lift up your head and call to Him in your normal voice. Go deep with God in prayer.

Perhaps you're asking, "How exactly do I go deep in prayer?"

You just do it. So often our biggest problem with this prayer thing is that we just never get untracked and rolling. As weird as it may sound, the reason this usually happens is that we're expecting everything and nothing from prayer at the same time. Let me explain.

Michael recently declared, "Dad, I don't think I'm praying right. It isn't working."

"Are you praying every night?" I inquired.

"Yes, I sure am," he answered.

"You're obeying God, then, right?"

"Yes, I am."

"Then it's working," I replied.

You see, on one level you may be expecting spiritual fireworks to explode in the sky the second you close your eyes. For Michael, there were no voices, no visions—no va-voom! To him, that meant nothing was working, but I'd seen some profound changes in his character from the time he began meeting with his Father each night. From my point of view, everything was working fine. Don't expect too much too soon.

But don't go in expecting nothing, either. You may go awhile dabbling along in prayer until you notice there's been little change in your level of intimacy with the Lord. *See? I knew prayer wouldn't work for me. Why should I press any harder?*

Let me speak plainly here. It won't be the guy who *believes* in prayer who will get that close connection with His Father. It will be the one who *prays* who will get that closer connection. You need to get started, and you need to keep going.

Seeking That Intimate Connection

When my pastor, Dave Olson, was a teenager, he was a rebellious kid heavy into drug and alcohol use. He got saved and entered a Christian treatment center called Teen Challenge, where he was freed from his drug and alcohol dependency. From the pulpit, he recently shared how hungrily he sought an intimate connection with the Lord when he was a young man:

When I graduated out of Teen Challenge, I kept attending their worship services to stay connected with my friends, but the center closed down nine months later. Everyone my age moved away, except for me.

So there I was alone—young, single, and very lonely. Those I did keep in touch with told me about their prayer life and how close they were to God. They told me I needed to seek Him.

Seek him? How do you do that? I wondered. I honestly didn't understand the terminology. All I knew was that I was desperate to connect with Him.

So late one night, I walked over to this big old church across from my apartment. The doors were still open, but no one was there. I didn't really know what to do, so I just walked around, saying out loud, "God, here I am! Your Word says You promised me abundant life, but I don't feel it. I want You to reveal Yourself to me, so here I am. Lord, I'm here!"

Nothing happened. My words reverberated inside the large sanctuary, but the lack of response didn't stop me from coming back. Night after night I'd come back to pray, saying in one way or another, "God, here I am. I'm asking You to move in my life."

Still nothing. I began to read the Bible at that church, too, even though I usually didn't understand a word I was reading. One night, however, I came across a passage about someone dancing before the Lord. So I looked around, even under the pews, to make sure no one else was inside the church, and I just started dancing and hopping around. After working up a bit of a sweat, I said, "Lord, there it is. I'm obeying Your Word. I'm asking You to answer. I'm asking You to move in my life."

Nothing changed. All I knew was to keep being obedient. I don't know how many weeks went by—maybe six or eight—but then there came a time when God began showing up. Wow!

As I kept on going to that church each night, He kept on showing up too. On one of those nights, I had the most holy moment I've ever had with Him. What an awesome experience. God promised me things about my future that I've never told another soul, and some have already come true.

These days I tell people that He'll show up for you if you just take Him at His word and be honest and humble with Him. Just say, "God, I don't understand this book, but I know it contains secrets to the universe. Lord, I'm asking You to open it up. I'm just going to begin reading it, and I want You to renew my mind. I want to be transformed."

You should get off alone and wait on Him in prayer, saying: "God, I'm setting the Bible aside for a while because that's just the menu. You, Lord, are the meal. God, here I am. God, please show up!"

You may not feel anything for weeks, but keep pressing in: "Lord, here I am, right back in Your face again. Lord, I'm taking You at Your word. You said that if I will soak in Your glory, I will be transformed, so come in Your glory, Lord."

If you begin to seek Him with all of your soul, God will honor what you're doing. He will transform you. If you are dissatisfied with your life or your walk with God or are hanging on to fears and insecurities, I'm telling you God does not want you to live there. He wants to deliver you and restore you. And don't forget that thirst you've had for more of God. He wants to quench that thirst too, but you've got to get into His presence.

Get into His presence. When it comes to prayer and connection, this is your first, simple goal. Just do it. It doesn't matter how much or how little you know about these things. I've read a few books on prayer over the years, but nearly everything important that I've learned about prayer came from the doing, not from the reading. The reading mainly helped me to understand what I was already experiencing.

When it first occurred to me to seek my Father with a regular prayer life, I knew little more than what Pastor Dave did. After all, my parents never prayed with me in our home, so I had never seen what it looked like. I had some ideas that I'd scrounged from a few sermons along the way, but for the most part, I had no idea where I was going. With few navigational clues, I idled on the taxiway, unable to take off. I burned a lot of fuel pondering how to get off the ground.

Then an idea popped into my head as I mulled my battle with sexual sin after my big moment on Merle Hay Road: *What if I just obeyed and got started? Maybe God will teach me about prayer as I go along, just as He taught me about purity.*

He had taught me so much during that battle for sexual purity. For instance, I learned that obedience is the opening whistle to play ball in God's kingdom. Nothing really happens until obedience starts.

Then I stumbled upon something that Oswald Chambers wrote in *My Utmost for His Highest* that really made things clear for me:

All God's revelations are sealed until they are opened to us by obedience. You will never get them open by philosophy or thinking. Immediately you obey, a flash of light comes.... Obey God in the thing He shows you, and instantly the next thing is opened up.

That's exactly how God began to open the truths about purity once I'd stepped out in obedience. The first thing He did was to remind me of what I'd read in my Human Sexuality 101 class back at Stanford—how men can draw sexual gratification through their eyes. So I began obeying God in this first thing He showed me. I began bouncing my eyes from joggers and sexy-dressed women.

Once I'd obeyed and confronted that first thing, He turned my attention to that second battlefront of the mind. One night I was driving on an Iowa road between Fort Dodge and Harcourt. The moon was full, the air was crisp and clear, and I was dreamy as I played with my thoughts about an old girl-friend of mine. A bit too directly, I guess, because the Lord broke in and said, *You have no right to any relationship of any type with this girl anymore, even in your thoughts.*

After I lost my short-but-fierce argument, the Lord began once more to faithfully open the next truth to me by bringing this Scripture verse to my attention:

We demolish arguments and every pretension that sets itself up against the knowledge of God, and *we take captive every thought to make it obedient to Christ.* (2 Corinthians 10:5)

I committed once more to obedience and stepped out to confront my thoughts about my ex-girlfriend by taking those thoughts captive and replacing them with songs and hymns.

Such examples confirmed that Oswald Chambers had been absolutely right when he said that it isn't your philosophizing or meditation that opens God's truth to you; it is your faithful step of obedience in spite of your lack of understanding.

That idea now changed everything in regard to prayer. I'd been wringing my hands on the runway with my prayer engines idling, wondering if I'd ever take off. But suddenly my problem with prayer seemed clear. Just as it had been in the battle for sexual purity, I knew I'd never learn a thing about prayer until I stepped out in obedience and got into His presence.

As I did, I counted on God to tell me where to go. He took me to scriptures that pointed out the people and things to pray for:

- my strength and obedience (Luke 22:40)
- my pastor (Ephesians 6:19)
- the lost (John 17:20)

- the found (Ephesians 6:18)
- my enemies (Luke 6:28)

I made a prayer list for each day of the week. For instance, my Thursday list contained the names of relatives and friends who didn't know the Lord. On Fridays I lifted up the needs of my enemies, including people who had recently attacked me.

I had certain friends or situations to pray for every day of the week. After a few months of going through my list and checking it twice, I tired of the whole thing, as it felt entirely like a one-way conversation. I figured I must be wasting my time and that God was bored silly by the entire exercise. I even thought I heard Satan chuckling at me from a distance. My heart was failing in its commitment, and my flesh was screaming for retreat.

What I didn't know was that the Lord was about to open the next truth to me. One morning I honestly prayed, "Lord, is this really a waste of time? If I'm off track, just tell me what to do next. Am I boring You with my many words? I really want to know what to do."

Out of nowhere I heard the instruction, *Look at Hebrews 9:6.* Where did that thought come from? I had no idea what that particular scripture said, but I was suddenly *very* curious to find out, so I snatched up my Bible and read:

> When everything had been arranged like this, the priests entered regu-
> larly into the outer room to carry on their ministry.

As I read it, the Holy Spirit simultaneously made His point: *It's okay to do the same things over and over again. The discipline of daily prayer and worship has been My plan from the beginning, starting way back with the priests.*

Wait a minute! I thought. *God gave me a Bible verse! Hey, we're talking!* I was so jazzed that I had no problem getting up in the morning to pray, although after a while it began to feel like a real grind to get through my list again. In fact, I was even beginning to feel a bit desperate about it. I didn't feel as though I was getting any closer to the Lord, and I told Him so.

"Lord, I've obeyed You each day," I offered. "You've just got to show me how to get closer to You! I know there has to be more to our relationship than this, Father. Would You please show me how to find You? Please, Lord! Please don't leave me like this!"

Shortly after that, I heard Charles Swindoll mention on his *Insight for Living* radio broadcast that he begins every time of prayer by singing praises to the Lord. "Without this, I just can't seem to connect with Him as well," he explained.

Hey, I can do that! I'd been memorizing hymns as part of my battle for sexual purity, and I knew a few popular worship choruses, so I started singing those songs before praying each morning. Amazingly, those songs opened my heart to deeper prayer from the get-go.

Once again, God had come through by revealing a new truth for me as I obeyed. Once again, I found that He was always listening because I am His child. I only need to press in with Him.

You need to press in with Him too. If prayer has been dry for you, it's probably because you haven't been worshiping beforehand. Remember, prayer is not for the purpose of getting God to do your will but for the purpose of aligning your heart with His. What can align your heart with His quicker than worship?

An additional key to experiencing God's heart in prayer is dumping your agenda overboard. I've heard it said that 90 percent of getting the revelation of God's plan for you is in sacrificing your heart completely to Him beforehand. In other words, you aren't asking to take a peek at His plan to see if you like it before you'll commit to it. Instead, you're willing to commit to His plans up-front, sight unseen.

Dueling agendas will never do in God's kingdom. They cause confusion, as you can see from Peter's e-mail:

I'm good friends with a young woman. We've talked about taking things to the next level, but she says she needs time for God to work in her life, meaning that she isn't ready to commit to me yet. I totally understand that, and the last thing I want to do is come between her and Jesus. But it's still hard, because I really want to have the chance to love, serve, and cherish her in marriage.

This is where the issue of motives confuses me. Is it right to pray to God and ask Him for her heart? Where does my honesty with God cross the line into selfishness as I'm begging Him to give me her hand in marriage?

Peter is asking valid questions here, and it's clear that he wants to put his own agenda in its proper place. What I've found is that when you first go to the Lord in worship before heading into prayer, your own agenda will naturally begin to fade into the background. As you worship Him regularly, you will begin to sense His beauty and His wisdom so intensely that only His agenda will matter anymore. His *glory* will become your agenda.

About a year before the idea of writing my first book, *Every Man's Battle,* had even entered my mind, a deep passion for the Lord's glory began to burn in my gut. I can remember driving the family to church and dropping Brenda and the kids at the front door. Nearly every time I walked across the parking lot that whole year, tears would pool, and my heart would groan under my breath. *Oh God! Give me a voice in Your kingdom! Please, God! It's burning me up inside! Give me a voice! I'm aching for the chance to speak for You. I don't care how small it is or how menial it all might be. Please, Lord, give me something to do for You!*

By the time I'd get to the door of the church, I'd be burning inside, tucking my head, and wiping the tears quickly so no one would see. But read my prayer again and notice something. I had no personal agenda but Him. I longed to bring Him glory, and I didn't care about the details.

So He gave me the idea to write *Every Man's Battle.* Now, if I'd been gripping my agenda tightly and demanding to know whether His plans matched up with my plans, I wouldn't have ever agreed to write an in-depth, public exposé about my sexual sin, I can assure you.

But God's eyes are always looking for the man with no agenda, the man who loves Him enough to volunteer for hazardous duty. If you want God's revelation in prayer and want His destiny for your life, dump your agenda, and, above all, don't fear His will. Remember, God's will is exactly what you would want for yourself if you knew all the facts as He does.

Now, seven years later, knowing the rest of the story, I realize that writing *Every Man's Battle* has been exactly the voice I'd been begging for, and I wouldn't trade what happened for anything in the world.

Go into worship! Seek His face in prayer. Ask Him to show you His way for you, that you might serve Him gratefully in spirit and in truth. By all means, go ahead and share the deepest dreams and concerns of your heart, but don't neglect the dreams and concerns of His heart.

You are His warrior. Find His heart. As you press on, you will find yourself shedding tears for the things that are on your Father's heart, and you will find your heart breaking over the things that break His heart.

Now, as long as we're speaking of worship, it's vital that you understand one-on-one worship with God if you ever expect to experience Him in that deeper way you desire.

For Personal Reflection

1. How has sin affected your prayer life over the years?

2. Ponder this question again from page 160: Are your prayer times with the Lord so intimate that they rock your emotions as deeply as sex or masturbation?

3. Why is your obedience to pray so crucial in learning about prayer?

4. I recently heard a worship leader urge us to cry, "Lord, make me a fool for you! I'll go anywhere, do anything!" Can we possibly mean that if we aren't even "fool" enough to go to our basements to pray regularly?

Experiencing the Father Through Worship

We were just young people who preferred the presence of God.
We were pursuing God. You'll never know your destiny
until you know the God who determined you.

—ANONYMOUS

When Charles Swindoll mentioned on his *Insight for Living* radio broadcast that he never prays without worshiping God first, he instantly vaporized all my paradigms regarding prayer.

Worship and prayer are connected? You mean you're supposed to worship God before you pray to Him? I'd been a Christian for more than six years, but these thoughts had never occurred to me.

What's more, the idea of worshiping God on my own was an even bigger bunker buster. Brenda was the strongest Christian I knew, but she didn't sing in worship before she prayed at home. She only worshiped God like that at church. As far as I could tell, everyone else I knew did that too. I know, of course, that the term *worship* covers far more than the act of singing. I know that *worship* can also broadly be used to define a guy's heart attitude toward God as he lives each day, for instance. But that "worshipful heart attitude" was hard to get my head around back then, and, besides, it hadn't yet launched me toward that new level of experience with God that I'd been craving.

Swindoll, on the other hand, had experienced something new and fresh, and he seemed to be saying, perhaps there's more to worship than you've ever dreamed, guys! Here's a simple step I've used. Gratefully, singing out loud before my prayer times was easy to grasp—yes, even for me—and taking a practical step outside my comfort zone seemed sensible too, since I wasn't all that comfortable with my spiritual life anyway.

So I tried his way of "worship first, pray second," and I'll describe what that looks like in a minute. But before I do, let me assure you of something right off. Swindoll was dead on the mark. There is more to worship than I'd ever dreamed, and if you've never worshiped the Lord regularly on your own, outside of church, then you haven't likely experienced some of the deeper levels of intimacy He would like to share with you. You were created to worship Him, and singing worship songs will usher you quickly into His presence. When I gave worship a big promotion in my daily walk with Him, the intimacy I felt in prayer and intercession jumped off the scale.

What's more, this kind of practical, one-on-one singing turned out to be the key to my permanent victory over sexual sin in my life. A thick growth of genuine intimacy with my Lord soon replaced my old desire for the false stuff from masturbation. When it comes to cementing your final victory in place, daily worship on the spiritual front of the battle will be every bit as important as bouncing your eyes and starving your sumo on the physical front, because it can convince your heart permanently just how much your Father loves you.

Here's how I got started that first morning. I pulled myself out of bed, brushed my teeth, got dressed, and walked downstairs to the basement. As a way to get started, I turned my palms slightly upward and began walking back and forth across the basement, quietly singing hymns and praise choruses I'd memorized. I beat a path across the carpet for about ten minutes, and then I knelt for about ten minutes of prayer time.

What happened on my knees was quite puzzling to me. The connection I sensed with the Lord when I prayed was…different…and better. Everything seemed to flow more naturally. For instance, I found it far easier to think of things to pray about while I knelt, and my ensuing prayer time didn't feel like work.

I thought for sure what happened that first day was a fluke, but it wasn't. The feeling of connection remained with me as I continued to worship God each morning. One day I plugged some of my favorite worship CDs into a boom box. That seemed to kick things up a notch further. As my passion for Jesus has grown through the years, these worship times have gotten stronger.

What kind of songs do I play in that boom box? Love songs! Songs I can sing *to* Him, songs that address *Him* directly. Let me explain. Many praise and worship songs are written in the third person, like this song based upon Psalm 24. I composed it as I agonized long into the night when Jasen was so sick in the hospital that I thought he might die by morning:

Who is this King? He's mighty in battle.
Who is this King? The Lord of Hosts!
He heals me and strikes at the heart of my enemy,
And He is Jesus my Lord.

Because of the circumstances surrounding this song, its message tugs deeply on my emotions, and the song means the world to me. But I would never use this song in my personal worship times with the Lord, no matter how much I love it. Why not? Consider whom I'm singing to when I sing this song. I'm not singing to Jesus but to my brothers and sisters in Christ.

There is nothing wrong with third-person songs like this, because they encourage us and strengthen our faith. Many third-person songs sweep my soul away and rock my heart peacefully in their harmonious chords. But when it comes to my personal worship times, third-person songs just don't cut it for me. I'm there for one thing and one thing only: I want to tell my Lord I love

Him, and I want to touch His heart in the way we both long for. Since I want to sing straight to Him from the deepest, most passionate corners of my heart, I use second-person love songs. Some of these I sing to the Father. Some I sing to the Son.

I've found countless songs like this that I can fire up during worship at home. One of my favorites goes like this:

> You're beautiful, altogether lovely.
> Forever I will be in love with You!

Another goes like this:

> I will worship You, my love,
> For taking every stain I wear and calling me beautiful.

Read those words again. Do you sense the yearning, the passion, the intimacy for Jesus in them? They have almost a romantic feel to them, like the kind of love songs you might sing to your girlfriend or fiancée.

None of this should surprise you. The Bible calls the church the bride of Christ, comparing His passion for us to a husband's devotion to his wife. But when I try to come up with the language to explain the intimacy I feel during my personal worship times with the Lord, I cannot. The words that come closest are "romance," "fascination," and "intoxication."

Nothing I've ever experienced beats the electricity of these moments with the Lord—the captivating touch, the deep passion, and the emotional tears you might expect in a love relationship but without any of the sensuality or self-focus that's part of relationships with females. It is all about Him and His overwhelming beauty. Your heart becomes one with His in these moments, and nothing else matters but Him.

This kind of intimacy is so vital in claiming long-term victory over sexual sin that it would be difficult to overstate it. Remember, masturbation is more of an intimacy issue than a sexual one, and it's often used to medicate pain and disconnection in your life, as this note from Brandon shows:

> I've been trying to stop masturbation by starving my sex drive. I've rooted out television from my life because it's been my biggest downfall, but I just can't get rid of masturbation. It's become so rooted in my life! I was on a mission trip recently, and I did it in my hotel room, and then as soon as I got home, I did it again. Is there any deeper advice you can give me to get through this problem? I know prayer is a huge factor, and I've prayed so much, but the masturbation is still there. I'm at a loss to know what to do.

Get into worship. That's my "deeper advice" to any guy in Brandon's situation. You've got to get connected, seek His face, and experience His presence. The more you worship, the more intimacy you'll have with Him. The more intimacy you have with Him, the stronger you'll stand against masturbation. That's why I believe worship is an even more important weapon on purity's battlefield than prayer. The passionate connection locks down a new, genuine companionship with God that replaces longing for the false kind that masturbation delivers.

Remember, I've said in the past that sexual intercourse transmits a genuine feeling of intimacy. False intercourse—masturbation—dishes out a similar sense of intimacy, but a counterfeit one. You need to replace the false intimacy of masturbation with this genuine intimacy with God.

Consider Kyle's story:

> Do you remember how I told you that my pastor prayed over me a few months ago, and I felt my bondage to sexual sin break as he prayed? Everything was going well until last night, when I was told at the last minute that the vehicle I was using to get to a men's retreat at the campground had stopped running. When that deep discouragement was

coupled with the sensual dreams I had last night, I felt so weak that I gave in and masturbated this morning. Now I feel like I've wasted the deliverance that the pastor's prayer brought to me.

Look, it isn't enough to be delivered. It isn't even enough to stand up with everything you've got and flee temptation on the physical battlefront. For permanent gains on the battlefield, you need to get tight with the Lord in worship.

That intimacy became a profound accountability partner in my life. As my passion for the Lord grew, He felt more and more real to me, and I could tell that those worship times with Him every morning meant as much to Him as they meant to me. As strange as this may sound, that passion became so real to me that it would no longer allow me to cheat on the Lord through the adultery of sexual sin. I just couldn't do that to Him. Besides, worship gives you such a loving ache for Him that you won't want to risk losing it by visiting some Web site or kicking back and watching Uma Thurman undress on the silver screen.

So get singing. If you live in a dorm, you'll have to get creative in finding a place to worship...maybe in the boiler room or the sanctuary of a nearby church. No matter where you have to go, find a place to be alone with the Lord. The Holy Spirit is waiting for you to step up to the plate, and He'll be there to help you. That's an ironclad promise.

False Notes

Before I turn you loose, you must understand a few things.

First of all, Satan hates your worship. He once led worship in heaven among the angels, and your worship reminds him of everything he's lost. He wanted to be equal with God. He wasn't satisfied with worshiping the King. You are satisfied, and that sets his hatred on edge.

I guarantee you that the Enemy doesn't want you to begin worshiping on your own, and he will surely try to stop you, using two of his primary assault weapons: *condemnation* and *pride.*

Now, condemnation *should* have little effect upon you. After all, condemnation is nothing but smoke and mirrors. Your Father says that condemnation no longer exists for you (see Romans 8:1), and the Word says Jesus was never about condemnation in the first place (see John 3:17). Satan can't condemn you. He is a far worse sinner than you've ever dreamed of being, so he has no room to berate you, and besides, he has no authority over you. Girls can't condemn you, because they have no experience by which to judge you. They aren't built like you, and it's quite likely that they have no clue what a ruthless battle your eyes can create for you. And as for us guys, which of us would have the gall to point the finger of condemnation at you when we're all pitching about in the same boat?

Since Calvary, only self-condemnation has any real power or life, and to extinguish that power, all you have to do is to quit hitting yourself on the head with that hammer of self-rejection. Self-condemnation may sound something like, *I'm no good. Intimacy with God won't happen for me, and my worship won't matter much to Him. He won't meet me there the way He meets everyone else.* Self-rejection can almost *feel* spiritual, but it is *not* spiritual. It is a lie.

But I know the real me beneath all His grace! Big deal! Do you think this great insight sets you apart as some kind of spiritual Einstein? We all know fully well what you would be if you didn't have Jesus in your life, but so what? The truth is, you *aren't* without Jesus, and you never will be again. You are a new creation, not that old one, and it won't do you any good to call God a liar about that day after day. You must accept the new truth about yourself. In other words, you must see yourself as the Lord sees you and walk in your new Christian identity. Train your mind through the Word. Be disciplined about it.

By all means, don't wait to stop masturbating before you reach out to Christ in worship and praise. You need that intimacy in your life. Toss your self-condemnation to the winds and run into His arms. His heart of passion longs for you. Worship Him. He's the Creator of the universe, and He's *for* you.

If you don't keep your eyes on that truth, self-condemnation will take you out as easily as the Enemy's more vicious weapon of pride. Keeping your eyes on the truth is always critical when dealing with Satan, because he's the father of lies, and all of his weapons are powered by deception.

When it comes to *pride,* I've run up against five "I don't have to worship alone" lies that play as Satan's nickel package in his defensive scheme in the worship arena. As your offensive coordinator, let me break down a few of the game tapes I've seen so you can recognize his defensive tendencies when you're in the midst of your heated skirmishes with him.

Deception No. 1: "I don't have to worship alone—it just feels too strange to do it."

I'll admit that, at first, it can feel very uncomfortable worshiping alone. I felt like a wild-eyed flake inside, and I was petrified someone would somehow see what I was doing in the basement each morning. I didn't even risk telling Brenda at first.

When Pastor Dave admitted that he had checked for people hiding under the pews before he started dancing in that big old church, I chuckled pretty hard. I knew that feeling only too well from my early days of worshiping alone in the basement. Before starting in, I'd peer out the basement windows to make sure no neighbors were peeking in and rolling their eyes, wondering, *What's that crazy loon up to this time?* Then, I'd tiptoe back to the stairs to make sure none of my kids had sneaked around the corner to spy on me and giggle. And I double-checked every few minutes just to make sure.

Even though the worship had an immediate effect on my prayer time, I almost quit the whole thing early on because I felt silly and self-conscious. It's hard for any man to consciously choose to look silly, even when no one is around. But I reminded myself that the Lord loves to hear love songs sung to Him, and I figured that as long as my hero Charles Swindoll was just as big a geek as I was, I couldn't be too far off the mark.

Though my prayer time improved immediately, I made little headway in sensing the Lord's presence during the first few weeks. But just as with Pastor Dave and his prayers at the church, suddenly the Lord responded, and things began to rock about the fourth week. Tears pooled regularly as I sensed His coming near each day, and soon my self-consciousness evaporated. As corny as it may sound, all I could see was Jesus. And as mystical as it might sound, worship must have transported me right into His throne room, because I could suddenly hear Him so much better than before.

Deception No. 2: "I don't have to worship alone—I like it better at youth group."

From my experience, young men and women stop short of getting alone with Him because it's far more comfortable for them to worship in a group setting at church.

But that kind of comfort can fool you. Perhaps all you've really done is learn what your prayers should sound like so that you can fit in with your peers. Or maybe you've learned to say the right words that seem to show a deep connection with Christ in order to make a name for yourself with the leaders.

I'll admit that you've got some great worship music to listen to—songs that light up your senses and give you an adrenaline rush. But if you're honest, you may have also noticed that this adrenaline high feels a lot like a Friday-night football game. Sure, you're feeling *something* during group worship. But is it a deep connection with God or a rush of emotion? The only way you can be sure you're connecting with Him in a group is to recognize that it's the same connection you sense with Him alone at home.

In fact, as paradoxical as it might sound, the key to praying and worshiping freely at church without self-consciousness is learning how to do it at home alone first.

When my youngest son, Michael, recently told me that he freezes up when he's put on the spot to pray in public, I told him he needed more practice.

"You mean I have to start volunteering to pray every chance I get at church? That sounds awful!" he moaned.

"No, I mean you need to pray more at home," I reassured him. "Logically, it *seems* that the best way to learn how to pray in public would be to practice more often in public." But I also explained to Michael that the key to praying in public without self-consciousness comes in making a tight connection with Christ. The best way to learn to make that kind of focused personal connection with Him, I said, would be to shut yourself off with Him at home. Then, when you're in public, it doesn't matter how big the crowd is or how wild the emotional chaos feels in your mind; you can still shut yourself away with Him and make that connection in the midst of everything.

"Your intimacy will be that great," I explained to Michael.

I'm not saying that worshiping and praying with others—like in a church or youth group setting—is a bad thing. (We call this corporate worship.) The Lord is enthroned upon the praise of His people, and there is so much spiritual power around us as we lift our hearts to Him together. But all that being said, if you aren't connecting on your own with the Lord in private, it is much harder to make a genuine connection with Him in the chaos of public worship.

Deception No. 3: "I don't have to worship alone—it feels too romantic."

Brad had this complaint to register:

> I can't sing any romantic love songs to God, because I don't feel it and
> am not sure I ever will. I certainly have no desire to pursue that feeling,
> if you know what I mean. I'm waiting for things to occur naturally
> instead.

What in the world does Brad mean when he writes that he wants worship "to occur naturally"? God commands you to seek Him actively with all of your heart, so if you are waiting for something to happen, you're out of line with His will. Besides, how long are you going to wait for this natural occurrence? One year? Five years? Ten years? For heaven's sake, you have the new life of Christ living in you! It's absurd to wait.

It's also unbiblical. Many real men were quite comfortable with intimacy in worship, including Enoch, Moses, David, Paul, and Silas.

Don't be arrogant about this romance issue, as Jay was when he wrote me this note:

> I hate it when these worship leaders pant, *I love you, God. I love you, Lord Jesus.* They say it the way you would say it to your sixteen-year-old girlfriend. They may be completely sincere, but I think they're just trying to show the rest of us how we are missing something so incredibly intimate and exciting.

Jay *is* missing out on something incredibly intimate and exciting. What more can I say? Don't be a fool regarding this "romance" issue, either. Don't cross your arms indignantly and snap, *I don't have to do this!*

Yes, you do. This is what you were created for, and if you are already wrapped up in a web of sexually addictive cords, that goes double. Just obey.

Evangelist Michael Brown once said that when he was single, he'd call all his friends on Saturday night to see what was happening, but on some of those nights they all had something going on—meaning he'd be home alone.

"It used to make my stomach churn with each successive phone call as it became clear that I'd have nothing to do and no place to go," he admitted. "I hated it, and I felt so alone, like some loser."

Then one night he heard God whisper, *Why not spend the evening with Me? I've got nothing going tonight.* The thought astounded Michael. Perhaps God had arranged for his friends to be busy so that he could spend some time with Him.

Hey, why not? I'm game, Lord! So Michael got out his Bible and worship tapes and began experiencing some of the most intimate, precious times he'd ever had with the Lord. "From that time forward," Brown said, "I never panicked when my friends were busy on the weekends. I'd just climb up into His arms and spend the evening with Him."

How's that for a different type of Saturday-night romance?

Deception No. 4: "I don't have to worship alone—that's not my thing, and besides, I'm too busy with work, school, or other activities."

That is an awful lie. It *is* your thing. In fact, it's your ministry:

> Now the Lord is the Spirit, and where the Spirit of the Lord is, there is
> freedom. And we, who with unveiled faces all reflect the Lord's glory,
> are being transformed into his likeness with ever-increasing glory.
> (2 Corinthians 3:17–18)

Moses would go up to the mountaintop, soak in the presence of God, and then he'd come down, and his face would literally be glowing as he spoke to the people. The apostle Paul says that this is what we are supposed to do so that with unveiled faces we may reflect the glory of God to those around us. God says in the next verse (4:1) that since we have this ministry, we should not lose heart.

What ministry? Answer: reflecting His glory! A large part of the ministry you're called to is simply to get in God's presence and to soak Him up. You are to spend time with Him until you're transformed by being with Him, and then you're to come off the mountain and shine among men. Any other ministry that doesn't include this element is dead, and you shouldn't want any part of it because it would not be a true ministry of the Spirit. The common element of real ministry—whether it's working on a community cleanup project or participating in a mission trip—is getting into His presence and soaking in His glory.

Before I speak to a large group, I try to spend at least ninety minutes in worship, soaking in His presence. Paul says that's how we're transformed from glory to glory, and if I want my words to transform others, I must first be transformed myself.

When a bloody Paul and Silas worshiped God from the depths of a dark, dingy Roman dungeon, God sent an earthquake (see Acts 16:25–26). God can use your worship to rock the spiritual strongholds in those around you in the same way, as He did with me in Benny's life:

I have been trying to live a righteous lifestyle, but my private devotional life has been dead. I never spent much time with God during the week, and at church I felt that praise and worship were just something to fill time before Pastor Ray gave his wonderful sermons. At the men's retreat on Saturday morning, your message about worship and intimacy with God really ripped me, and everything finally made sense. How could I expect to have true intimacy with my fiancée if my heart was hardened toward God? How could I hate my sin if I'm not one with God?

Your discussion of individual and family worship bore witness in my spirit, and I knew I had to change. On Sunday morning I was an usher assigned to the front, so I got to see you worship up close. It's obvious that your relationship with God is very deep and passionate. Seeing you demonstrate what you had just spoken about the day before showed me what I was missing. I just *had* to have more of God, which caused an uncontrollable urge to worship to come over me. I've been a Christian most of my life, but I've never had a worship breakthrough like this before.

If you're not spending time soaking in His presence in worship and cultivating that relationship, then you're not living in the center as a believer in Christ. You won't be transformed the way God desires.

Deception No. 5: "I don't have to worship alone—I'm just not there yet."

Barry wrote:

I do nothing more than mumble along when we sing songs like "All of my days I will sing of your greatness!" Those are the songs that tell God how faithful I'll be to Him…. I can't be that dishonest. I know me.

Sure, you know yourself well *today.* But worship transforms you, remember? Give God a couple of weeks of worship, and you will change—and you may not know yourself so well anymore. You might sing those songs with more honesty because you will be different.

Worship changes you, and a lot of young guys need plenty of change. Have you ever seen the jocks in their game jerseys leaning against the lockers with their hands in their pockets, looking cool as the girls flit around them like birds? I hated that kind of arrogance even when I was a jock.

Sadly, I often see young men with that same "sophisticated" look of arrogance standing in the middle of youth-group worship, hands in pockets, barely singing if at all. Their whole body language drawls, "Wassup? Yeah, baby, I'm cool with Jesus. He's my homeboy, and we've got an understanding. You know what I mean? I'm cool and He's cool."

Look, baby, Jesus isn't just cool. He's Lord. The days of prideful worship must be over in your life if you want sexual purity. You must throw your whole heart His way, at home and in public.

Become a real man. As the great evangelist Smith Wigglesworth once said:

> Praise is God's sunlight in the heart. It destroys sin germs. It ripens the
> fruits of the Spirit. It is the oil of gladness that lubricates life's activities.
> There can be no holy life without it. It keeps the heart pure and the
> eye clear. Praise is essential to the knowledge of God and His will. The
> strength of a life is the strength of its song. When the pressure is heavy
> that is the time to sing. Pressure is permitted to strengthen the attitude
> and spirit of praise. It takes a man to sing in the dark when the storm
> and battle are raging, and it is such singing that makes the man.

Satan's fear is that you'll finally see the connection between your worship and the Lord's power. You see, worship is not just about intimacy. It's also about a download of supplies to you—a download of wisdom and of strength.

On one recent Sunday night I felt weak and discouraged. I had one week left to meet my deadline for *Tactics,* and I still had six chapters to go. I was burned out and exhausted.

So I went into a time of worship with Brenda, and it was as if God stuck the hose of a gas pump through my ribs and pulled back on the handle. I could literally feel the strength pouring into me. The next morning, in great peace, I wrote this very chapter you're reading. His promises are true:

> Dwell in Me, and I will dwell in you. [Live in Me, and I will live in you.] Just as no branch can bear fruit of itself without abiding in (being vitally united to) the vine, neither can you bear fruit unless you abide in Me.
>
> I am the Vine; you are the branches. Whoever lives in Me and I in him bears much (abundant) fruit. However, apart from Me [cut off from vital union with Me] you can do nothing. (John 15:4–5, AMP)

I used to toss this "vine and fruit" language away as little more than a bouquet of flowery poetry. But it's not. Worship is your supply line, your most critical source of authority in the spirit realm. Worship will make you a real man to be reckoned with on any battlefront.

So remember, the key to deepening your prayer life and your intimacy with God is worship. If you want to be transformed in Him, you must soak in Him.

For Personal Reflection

1. Have you regularly connected individual worship with your individual prayer times over the years?
2. Does it surprise you to hear that worship has such an impact upon your prayer life? Why shouldn't it surprise us?
3. In your own words, explain why second-person songs—those that use the pronouns *you* and *your* for Christ—are more personal than third-person songs in your private worship times.
4. How does personal worship replace the need for the false intimacy of masturbation and porn?
5. Which of the five deceptions listed in this chapter are you most prone to?

15

Experiencing the Father Through His Word

> When the priests withdrew from the Holy Place,
> the cloud filled the temple of the LORD.
> And the priests could not perform their service
> because of the cloud,
> for the glory of the LORD filled his temple.
>
> —1 KINGS 8:10–11

Now, there was an experience with God!

I've been fortunate to experience God's glorious presence in ways that were just as unmistakably powerful as what the priests in God's holy temple felt that day. I've also heard God deliver personal messages to me directly through the Holy Spirit. But in spite of all of these wonderful moments, it's still true that the most common—and richest—way that God has "spoken" to me through the years has simply been through regularly reading His Word.

That statement may not prompt a fireworks display, and it may even disappoint you a little. Maybe Bible reading isn't exactly the kind of experience you have in mind when you dream of experiencing God.

If so, you've forgotten that the Bible is the Word of God. The Bible is a living document and extremely active in shaping the thoughts and attitudes of your heart (see Hebrews 4:12). Recall, too, that Jesus is the Living Word of God, in the flesh (see John 1:14). Therefore, an encounter with the Bible is an encounter with Jesus.

This point is so critical to understand. You will always be as close to God as you want to be, and the simplest way to get close to Him is through His written Word. Every time you crack open a Bible, you are getting into His presence. If you want to be close to the Lord, you must seek these Scripture encounters with Him with all of your heart.

When you read the Bible regularly, you grow in your knowledge of the Lord and learn exactly who God is:

> And we pray this in order that you may live a life worthy of the Lord
> and may please him in every way: bearing fruit in every good work,
> growing in the knowledge of God. (Colossians 1:10)

Just as important, the Bible teaches you who *you* are and how you're stacking up against your new knowledge of God. The Holy Spirit accomplishes this by springing pop-quiz questions at you while you're reading. A while back He hit me with these as I read Hebrews 13:

> Remember your leaders, who spoke the word of God to you. Consider
> the outcome of their way of life and imitate their faith. (verse 7)

Pop-Quiz Question No. 1: *Fred, since you are a Christian, you are also a leader like these men were. Have you considered the outcome of your lifestyle these days? Is it worthy to be imitated?*

At the time I was struggling with a bad case of bitterness, which I'll tell you more about in the next chapter. I'd swept it under a rug, but now the Spirit was tugging on that lumpy mess to bring it out into the light.

He landed His second blow when I read further in Hebrews:

Pray for us. We are sure that we have a clear conscience and desire to
live honorably in every way. (13:18)

Pop-Quiz Question No. 2: *Fred, are you sure you have a clear conscience?
Do you really desire to live honorably in every way or just in the easy ways?*

A few days later the Holy Spirit landed three more blows with some verses
I "stumbled upon":

> And this is my prayer: that your love may abound more and more in
> knowledge and depth of insight, so that you may be able to discern
> what is best and may be pure and blameless until the day of Christ,
> filled with the fruit of righteousness that comes through Jesus Christ—
> to the glory and praise of God. (Philippians 1:9–11)

Pop-Quiz Questions Nos. 3, 4, and 5: *Fred, is your love abounding more
and more in knowledge and depth of insight? Are you as pure and blameless today
as you hope to be on that day of Christ? Does the fruit of righteousness in your life
pour forth limitless praise and glory to God?*

These were tough questions to ask a bitter man, to be sure. See what I
mean by opening the Book and being immediately in the Lord's presence?
God confronts your belief system with the Word, which is painful. But in
doing so, He also renews your mind wonderfully:

> Do not conform any longer to the pattern of this world, but be trans-
> formed by the renewing of your mind. Then you will be able to test
> and approve what God's will is—his good, pleasing and perfect will.
> (Romans 12:2)

When you make the Bible a regular part of your life and get into His presence through those pages, the Lord uses His own image and example to keep
you on the straight and narrow and show you the right path:

Do not lie to each other, since you have taken off your old self with its practices and have put on the new self, which is being *renewed in knowledge in the image of its Creator.* (Colossians 3:9–10)

Your mind needs constant renewing because sometimes it forgets, especially in the heat of the moment. Like the time a few years ago when a guy rudely cut me off on—yes, you guessed it—Merle Hay Road. I decided immediately to set things right by cramming my foot to the floor and roaring back in front of him.

Brenda and the kids looked at me with bug eyes. "I hate it when you do that!" Brenda exclaimed. "It scares me to death, and besides, it sets a horrible example for the kids."

"If you are so worried about how we look in front of the kids, why are you attacking me in front of them?" I shot back. "I thought we agreed not to do that!"

"Like that absolves you of your actions!" she responded sharply. "Don't change the subject on this!"

"I've driven a ton of miles in my life, and I've never had one accident that was my fault," I explained smugly. "When a guy cuts me off like that, I'm only trying to get back in front of him quickly, because that makes him less dangerous to me. That's how I stay safe on the road!"

"If the safety of our family is your only concern, why did you make that ugly face at him when you roared by?"

"Look, he's an idiot, and he needs to know that, or he'll do the same thing to everyone else," I said dismissively. "But that's not the real point here anyway. I'm a man. I do billions of things at home exactly the way you want them done, but when it comes to driving, I'm going to do it my way. Leave me alone."

As Frank Sinatra sang one time, "I did it myyyyyy way."

Don't worry. You don't have to tell me I acted like an idiot. The Holy Spirit told me that Himself a few days later when He laid a small scripture before me:

A fool shows his annoyance at once,
> but a prudent man overlooks an insult. (Proverbs 12:16)

God's Word said it all: *A fool shows his annoyance at once!* That phrase is a perfect description of road rage, and "fool" was the perfect description of me. The *world* had taught me that real men rule the road. The Lord was using the *Word* to confront that wrong belief system. His obvious message was, *Prudent men overlook insults, even on the road.* Chastened and chastised, I apologized to Brenda and told the kids what I'd learned about myself.

Confronting Our Belief Systems

We have all kinds of beliefs and justifications that need to be confronted, especially in our sexuality:

- Real men look at the babe in the string bikini walking by on the beach!
- It's our right to stare at women! God made women beautiful so that we could enjoy His creation.
- Just because I don't get to order doesn't mean I can't look at the menu.
- Men are made this way.
- I'm a guy, and looking is a guy thing, so there's nothing wrong with treating myself to a little eye candy!

The Spirit actively confronts your belief system when you experience the Lord's presence through the Word:

With eyes full of adultery, they never stop sinning;…they are…an accursed brood! (2 Peter 2:14)

"Eyes full of adultery" means that these men desired every woman they saw and viewed each as a potential sex partner. "They never stop sinning" means that their eyes served as a constant instrument of lust. Sound familiar?

I used to believe I was just being a normal guy when I enjoyed my surroundings. God, though, said I was being part of an "accursed brood."

The more I got into His presence through the Word, the more He confronted me:

> Death and Destruction are never satisfied,
>> and neither are the eyes of man. (Proverbs 27:20)

The Lord critiqued my mind-set because He wanted to renew it; He wanted to bring it back to normal. He was saying, *Fred, right now your eyes are as insatiable as death and destruction.* I didn't like the sound of that at all. What's more, I thought I had shuttled my sexual sin issue to a side alley, where it wouldn't affect the rest of my spiritual life, but He confronted me regarding that attitude as well:

> If anyone turns a deaf ear to the law,
>> even his prayers are detestable. (Proverbs 28:9)

God confronted me because He loves me. If He hadn't done that, who would have? Brenda couldn't have confronted me, because she didn't know about my sin. The world couldn't have, because it doesn't have the truth. In fact, the world is so full of deception that it will accommodate and affirm your wrong beliefs at every turn.

That's why the Word is your only lifeline to normal. You've got to regularly hear a voice calling to you from another world, because no one here can do it for you. You've got to be in His presence so He can challenge you, even it it's only for fifteen minutes a day.

The most important thing I've ever done spiritually—besides learning how to worship in my basement—was committing to read my Bible from Genesis to Revelation in one year. When I first started following Christ, I was stunned to learn how few Christians had ever read the Bible from cover to cover. I thought, *These people are staking their eternity upon the truths of a book they've never even read all the way through!*

These days, it's really easy to read the Bible in one year, thanks to special editions that give you several chapters from the Old Testament, a few chapters from the New Testament, and a quick passage from Psalms and Proverbs for each day on the calendar. It takes ten or fifteen minutes to read, and by the end of the year, you'll have read both the Old and New Testament and reached your goal.

Language and Knowledge

Why is it so important to read the complete Bible? For a moment, perhaps it would be useful to think of the Bible as the "language of the Holy Spirit" rather than the "Word of God." When it comes to learning any language, knowledge of new words and common usages breeds more knowledge, doesn't it?

To learn German, for instance, you would start by learning a set of basic words and phrases—perhaps numbers one through ten, the days of the week, and simple phrases like "How are you doing?" and "Where's the bathroom?" At first, you're doing nothing more than accumulating the basic building blocks of the language so you can use them in elementary conversation.

Because of that, at times your German classes will seem dreary and boring. It takes time before you can utilize your limited vocabulary in a useful conversation and longer still before you can actually think in German. Fluency often requires a period of full immersion in the language by living in a German-speaking community.

The same is true regarding the language of the Holy Spirit. If you expect to learn His language, you need to build a vocabulary by reading the whole Bible on some sort of schedule, understanding that the building blocks of knowledge will breed more knowledge as you go along. That is why it's good to have a daily Bible-reading schedule.

Parts of the Bible will seem boring the first time you read them, because you don't have the necessary "language skills" for complete understanding. On those days, you may not learn anything but the building blocks, which is fine, because you're accumulating information for the Holy Spirit to use with you later.

Don't be surprised if there are days when you don't understand a single thing you're reading; that's just part of learning the language. Stay with it, because God will open things up into "fluency" as you increase your vocabulary.

That's exactly how it happened for me. About halfway through my *second* reading through the Bible, it felt as though the sun broke through the clouds. Or, to describe it in language terms, I was starting to form my own "sentences." For instance, as I read Psalms the second time around, I could begin to place some of them in their context within Jewish history.

God even began to use obscure, boring texts to impact my life greatly. For instance, read these plain-vanilla verses, but pay attention to the italicized line:

Greet Mary, who worked very hard for you.
Greet Andronicus and Junias, my relatives who have been in prison
    with me. They are outstanding among the apostles, and they
    were in Christ before I was.
Greet Ampliatus, whom I love in the Lord.
Greet Urbanus, our fellow worker in Christ, and my dear friend
    Stachys.
Greet Apelles, tested and approved in Christ.
Greet those who belong to the household of Aristobulus.
Greet Herodion, my relative. (Romans 16:6–11)

I remember being stopped dead in my tracks by that line about Apelles. *Wow! The great apostle Paul knew this guy personally and deemed him tested and approved of Christ. I want that to be said of me!* Later I used that single line to create a strong lesson on purity for my Sunday-school class.

By then, obviously, I was more fluent in the language. Once that had happened, the Holy Spirit could tap me in the middle of the day and say things like, *Remember the time Jezebel told Ahab to steal that vineyard? Can you see how that story parallels this business deal you are working on?*

That's what I mean about reading all of Scripture and becoming fluent in the language of the Holy Spirit so He can reveal information to you. Once you know the language, the Holy Spirit can be twice as active in your life. He can still speak to you while you're *physically* reading your Bible, but He can also speak to you in that same language at any time, day or night.

I've heard well-meaning people say, "Just get into the Bible and read a little to experience it. If you don't understand a part or find it boring, just skip over it." Others may say, "It's better to read three verses and camp there for a week than to read ten chapters and not know or remember a thing."

Both points of view are valid, but that doesn't mean volume is a negative thing, either. Don't use those positions as excuses to avoid immersing yourself in the language. On a consistent basis, read through the entire Bible—and then start over again. (*The One Year Bible* by Tyndale House, which uses the New Living Translation, is an excellent resource.)

But how can Christ be free to move in my life if I'm on a schedule? Doesn't that box Him into a corner? I used to worry about the same thing, but I needn't have. It amazes me how God finds ways to time certain chapters to the very day I need to read them, in spite of my schedule.

In the last chapter I told you how I composed a song the night I thought Jasen might die. Here are the lyrics again:

Who is this King? He's mighty in battle.
Who is this King? The Lord of Hosts!
He heals me and strikes at the heart of my enemy,
And He is Jesus my Lord.

But now...the rest of the story. A few days before Jasen became ill, I had added five psalms a day to my Bible-reading schedule in order to finish the book of Psalms in one month. I was breezing through Psalm 21–25 without a care until I was stopped cold by Psalm 24, especially these verses:

> Who is the King of glory?
> The LORD strong and mighty,
> The LORD mighty in battle.
> Lift up your heads, O gates,
> And lift them up, O ancient doors,
> That the King of glory may come in!
> Who is this King of glory?
> The LORD of hosts,
> He is the King of glory. Selah. (Psalm 24:8–10, NASB)

I had no idea why those verses made such an impression on my heart. Everything in my life seemed in perfect order, and yet I felt compelled to read those verses over and over again.

Then, later that morning, a phone call came from Brenda. "The school called and said Jasen is very sick. Meet me at home right away. I'm going to get him now."

When I had given Jasen a hug that morning, he was fine. When Brenda brought him home at noontime, however, he had a baseball-size growth sticking out of the side of his neck. We were shocked. My wife frantically rushed him to the hospital while I stayed home with the girls and crumpled to the floor in terror and prayer.

After examining Jasen, the emergency-room doctors were quite concerned. They said it appeared that a strep infection had passed Jasen's throat and settled in the lymph nodes. If they couldn't quickly stop the growth of the bacteria, the swelling nodes would cut off air through his windpipe. Jasen would not be able to breathe.

After a medical team ministered to and treated Jasen all afternoon and into the evening, I sang and rocked Rebecca to sleep while my spirit clung to the words of Psalm 24 that I had half memorized that morning. After tucking her in, I wrote that first verse of my song.

The whole experience floored me. *Wow! God prepared me ahead of time with this psalm! He knew this was coming later that morning and wanted to comfort me even before I knew about it!*

By the next morning, the danger had passed, and the doctors said Jasen would make a full recovery. As I headed downstairs and read the next five psalms on my schedule, I came to these verses from Psalm 30:

O LORD my God,
I cried to You for help, and You healed me....

O LORD, by Your favor You have made my mountain to stand strong....

You have turned for me my mourning into dancing;
You have loosed my sackcloth and girded me with gladness,
That my soul may sing praise to You and not be silent.
O LORD my God, I will give thanks to You forever. (Psalm 30:2, 7,
        11–12, NASB)

I was so thrilled by God's goodness that I felt I could have written the psalm myself. In fact, later that night I took those words and did just that, writing the second verse of the song as Rebecca slept on my shoulder once more:

He turns my mourning to dancing,
And He girds me with gladness and song!
By His favor, my mountain stands strong o'er my enemy
That my soul may sing praise to Him!

You can't convince me that a read-the-Bible-in-one-year schedule is little more than a dead set of rules and ritual. I can tell you story after story of times when God used my day's scheduled reading for a specific issue that day. Even when I'd missed a few days of Bible reading, I found that what I was reading that day was *exactly* what I needed—even though I was behind on my schedule! Whatever was happening, I learned that God's Word is never dead. It's alive.

How does He do it? I don't know. All I know is that the Bible is our source of truth, and the Lord is our source of strength. As long as we are getting into His presence regularly through the Word, He will find a way to use it to bring life to us and glory to Himself.

Combination Platter

To experience God fully, you need to soak in His presence through prayer and worship, and you need to be renewed in His presence by His Word. As you begin to incorporate all three disciplines into your life, your connection will be so tangible and intimate that He'll be able to both comfort you and transform you during the roughest times.

A few years back I received an early evening phone call from my sister Pennee. She'd just found Dad dead on his living-room couch, where it appeared he had died peacefully while taking a nap.

The next few days became a blur of conflicting emotions. It was no family secret that Dad and I had not had the best relationship. On one hand, his death brought a welcome peace to me. After all, he had never accepted me as a man nor accepted Brenda as a worthy part of the family. I couldn't help being relieved that I'd never hear him angrily curse me or my wife again.

Still, he was my father, and I loved him in spite of everything. I'd spent many an afternoon during the last two years of his life trying to rebuild a relationship that had gone sideways. I knew that he had enjoyed seeing me as he shuffled slowly toward his death, and I felt the same way.

Because of the mixed feelings, I made it through the funeral without a serious emotional breakdown. Even when Dad's lawyer got a bit nasty with me after the burial and reminded me that I had been cut out of my father's will,

I wasn't bothered. After all, that was very old news. He had cut me out of his will a dozen years earlier, and that was fine with me. I didn't want his money if he didn't want to give it to me.

But that afternoon as I left his hometown of Keystone, Iowa, to head back to Des Moines and rejoin my family, I drove past the local cemetery and saw the pile of dirt by his burial site. Without warning, my emotions ambushed me like a huge tsunami.

It had suddenly occurred to me what it really meant to be struck from Dad's will, and it had nothing to do with money. Dad wanted me to know that right down to his last breath, he didn't consider me worthy to carry the Stoeker name.

I can't explain very well what happened inside as that truth barreled into my heart, but it was as awful as anything I can remember. I could barely catch my breath as my sobs wrenched my stomach and chest. The highway blurred with tears, and when I made a desperate call to Brenda for help, I couldn't talk for long because my crying was relentless.

At that moment the years of practicing all three spiritual disciplines came together into one of the more beautiful connections I'd ever experienced with my Lord. I flipped in a worship CD and played a comforting worship song called "Precious Pearl."

I turned to the Lord and rasped in prayer, *Father, I'm dying inside. Please help me!* Another wave of crushing emotion crashed over me and choked off my prayer. I could barely hear the song above my crying, but somehow the lyrics found their way into my consciousness and reminded me of the truth that I needed to hear:

My flesh and my heart may fail,
> but God is the strength of my heart
> and *my portion forever.* (Psalm 73:26)

The prayer, worship, and the Word buried in the lyrics of this song combined to deliver the comfort I needed, but it didn't stop there. The Lord

Himself said, *Don't be dismayed, my son. I will personally be your inheritance and not the kind the world gives. No one will ever take this inheritance away from you because I love you, and that won't change. Your dad didn't think you were worthy to carry his name, but I'm very proud to have you carry my name, Son.*

Talk about turning my mourning to dancing and my sadness to song! My friend, no one can do it as He can.

Get into His presence.

Seek His face with all your heart.

And experience your Father in all His grace and glory.

For Personal Reflection

1. Are you regularly allowing your belief systems to be rocked by the Lord's pop quizzes in the Word?
2. Why is the Word of God your only lifeline back to normal?
3. What has kept you from learning the language of the Spirit in the past?

A WARRIOR'S CHALLENGE

Alex seemed a bit edgy on the other side of the breakfast table, but Ruben fixed his gaze on him anyway. "Alex, what is life to you? What does it all mean?"

Alex fumbled with his pancakes as he floundered for a decent answer. Finally his eyes locked on to Ruben's. "I don't have a clue," Alex admitted. "It's not about making money, at least not for me. It's not about marrying, although that sure would be nice. It's not about eating, and it's not even about all the sexual stuff. I just don't know. I feel so stuck in my life right now—I'm almost numb. I just want to collapse. Why does it all matter?"

First of all, life matters because you are God's son, and He needs you to be about His business. It matters because your destinies are intertwined, and He's counting on you to help Him draw the lost ones into the family.

When a guy with no relationship with Jesus Christ sees authentic transformation in a young man, something deep within him leaps up and cries, *That's what I want too!* A changed heart always draws men to Christ, and why not? Who wouldn't want the abundant life, that wild adventure that only God can promise and fulfill? The second reason that life matters—and the second half of the Great Commandment—lies in meeting the challenge of loving our brothers as we love ourselves. What man doesn't long to fight for right in the lives around him? We are born to be heroes in Him and for them.

I'll admit there is great satisfaction in mano a mano, hand-to-hand combat with Satan, as Manny will attest:

> I was getting ready for bed, and my roommate was gone. Just then, the devil filled my thoughts with lust and all my weaknesses. I was beginning to act on the thoughts when I suddenly realized that this was a test. I immediately stopped what I was doing and rebuked the devil in the power of Jesus's name. Then, I prayed, rolled over, and fell asleep. That victory was an amazing rush.

I've found, though, that it's an even bigger rush when you fight for God's purposes in your brother's life and for his freedom to live for his own audience of One. It comes as you begin to see yourself as God sees you—His partner in destiny, His brother in arms. It comes as you focus on the body of Christ and not your body alone:

> Therefore, strengthen your feeble arms and weak knees. "Make level paths for your feet," so that the lame may not be disabled, but rather healed. (Hebrews 12:12–13)

Sure, you must start by strengthening your own weak knees, but you won't be finished until you heroically help heal the lame brothers limping at your side. Only then will your Father's family flourish, and only then will you have lived a destiny that matters. The picture is clearing for Keith:

> I've committed to stop masturbating and to replace that desire with intimacy with God and with my Christian brothers around campus. I

can't express how free I feel and, surprisingly, how much more manly I feel. God has renewed my mental image of manhood to be that of a warrior who fights for his King, and as a result, my self-image has improved dramatically.

For the rest of this book, we'll discuss how to broaden your vision, which will define your destiny as His son and warrior.

16

Understanding the Game

Make every effort to live in peace with all men and to be holy;
without holiness no one will see the Lord.
See to it that no one misses the grace of God
and that no bitter root grows up to cause trouble and defile many.

—HEBREWS 12:14–15

A blameless, obedient life is a blessing to others because it draws men to Christ. It's also a blessing to you:

When God raised up his servant, he sent him first to you *to bless you by turning each of you from your wicked ways.* (Acts 3:26)

But this begs an important question: if complete obedience is so good for everyone around us, why do we fight it so hard?

Well, let's be honest about it. The spiritual game is a tough one. You certainly want to fight for right in the lives around you, but not everyone sees you as their hero while you're doing it, and sometimes you feel more like a frustration to them than a blessing. Meeting your Father's challenge to love your brothers like yourself will require genuine maturity on your part. Welcome to the game, man.

The first thing to understand about this game is that God's power sets off relational earthquakes whenever it touches you. When His transforming power rocks your world, repentance will rumble, and deep changes will roll across your soul's landscape, registering smaller seismic disturbances in everyone and everything you touch. Relational earthquakes are natural occurrences in the kingdom of God.

You may have experienced at least one massive quake in your life—I'm talking about salvation. I'll never forget when God shook my world. One day I was the Soto Hall beer-chugging champion at Stanford. The next time you saw me, I wasn't drinking anymore. One day I was swapping porn magazines with my buddies. The next time they saw me, I was reading my Bible in the park. Do you suppose my friends were uncomfortable around me for a while? I'm afraid so. They had no idea what nasty bug had bitten me.

Sadly, it's this relational component that can stop you from capitalizing on these encounters with God and translating them into a changed lifestyle. The initial earthquake is never the problem, because it originates from the loving hand of your Father. The real problems arise when the relational aftershocks come rolling through your life.

For every change you make, there will be a challenge to that change within your relationships. All of us have our comfort zones, and none of us likes to have change imposed upon us. There, of course, lies the rub, because whenever you change, you simultaneously impose that change on everyone in your relational grid. "Gee, guys, what do we do with an alcohol-free Fred? Do we invite him along tonight? Will he still be fun, or will he just drone on and on about what God has been doing in his life?"

There seems to be only one logical way to eliminate these aftershocks. Since you set them in motion with your decision to change, the way to stop them is to reverse that same decision. If the natives get more and more restless with the effects of that change upon your relationships, what will you do? All I know is that if you don't give everyone a chance to adapt to this new you by pressing through these conflicts to the end, the new you will quickly vanish.

Maybe you've seen it happen before. Your lukewarm Christian buddy heads off to a retreat, gets blasted by God, and comes back on fire…until the next weekend on campus. When the going gets tough—and it usually does—he nestles right back into his old spot in the relational grid instead of pressing through so that those changes can impact others.

This dynamic lives in every relationship. Once you upset the roles and rules in a relationship, even the godly people who love you—who want you tight with God—start applying the pressure to dial down your "radicalism."

What keeps many men from pressing through during these times is the fear of how it might affect their relationships. There are people whom you love and respect, and you desire their approval. Sometimes—when the conflict poses too high a relationship risk—you'll downshift for the sake of that person. In tears, Danny once told his mother, "It's hard to be a Christian with Dad because he wants me to watch television with him, and it's always the stuff you don't like, Mom. He always gets mad at me if I won't watch those shows with him." Now seventeen, Danny has relaxed his movie standards for the sake of that relationship with his dad. Naturally, he is struggling hard with his purity, but he won't talk to his dad about the things they are watching, because he's afraid of losing the relationship.

Spiritual change usually creates earthquakes in human relationships, and there is nothing you can do about it except deal with it. If you want to go deeper with God in intimacy and purity, the wise way to proceed is to make the following decision at the outset: "I don't care how anybody responds to my new walk of purity, because I'm going all the way with Jesus. It doesn't matter how much conflict it produces in my relationships, either. We'll just work through any conflict."

Notice that I didn't say the following: "I'm going all the way with Jesus, and if people don't like it, they can just stick it up their nose!" Sure, you've got to press through during these rumbling relational times, but I'm not talking about becoming a finger-pointing grouch, a haughty blow-hard, or a bull in a china closet—in other words, a jerk.

You must be loving and humble even when others advise you to rein in your passion for Jesus. You just can't afford to dial things back. Remember, you are God's son, and your family destiny is intertwined with His. You are His agent of change in your branch of His family tree.

God brings His kingdom to earth through every one of us. He'll change you, which will ripple change into every sphere of your influence. That's how God cleans up His family tree and how He takes over the world.

God's not unhappy with all these ripples and aftershocks. In fact, that's why God gives you a fresh touch in the first place. No matter how comfortable you become in your relational network, He's usually tired of the status quo. He wants to change you so He can change others around you. Take a look at how He's using Jeremy:

> The guys at my lunch table saw me reading *Every Young Man's Battle* and said, "Are you kidding us, Jeremy? Do you really believe you can do this?"
>
> I didn't know what to say, so I just turned toward them and gave them a wan smile. Eddie blurted, "Jeremy, get a clue, buddy! It's a natural process!"
>
> There was my opening, so I took a deep breath and explained a lot of your principles to them. I was surprised when they began listening carefully.
>
> Afterward Sully responded, "So, you're saying that if a girl bent over to pick up a book, you wouldn't look? Jeremy, come on! It's not your fault! Her rear end is like a magnet!"
>
> "Of course it is," I said. "But just because you are made that way doesn't mean you have to stay that way."
>
> Anyway, we eventually moved on to class, but I found out later that one of the girls sitting nearby was listening to our conversation. As we were passing in the hallway, she grabbed my arm and pulled me over to the side. "I really respect what you are doing," she said. "I wish those guys knew how much I agree with everything you told them! I really admire your determination in this, Jeremy."

I was blown away and not just because I hadn't realized she had been listening. It was because of the intent look in her eye and the way she said it.

I admire Jeremy to no end. When his Father freshly revived his purity and dropped the new Jeremy off at school, the young man bravely walked onto campus knowing full well he wouldn't fit in as he had before. Jeremy didn't conform so that he would be accepted, and he didn't backslide into his old relational matrix. He stood his ground and stood for righteousness. Some of those around Jeremy admired him for what he said. Some didn't.

But that doesn't faze God in the least. The only line in His ledger that matters is the bottom one: Jeremy was out there being about his Father's business, and his brand-new life was impacting his Father's family tree. Those guys at the table were confronted by the truth of God, and the next time they look at a girl's rear end, an aftershock of disturbance will roll across their hearts.

An Example in Spades

Everything will break loose as you move deeper with God. That's a given. All God is asking of you is that you endure these relational conflicts so you can point His lost children home toward His truth and encourage your sisters and brothers by your example. Jeremy was doing both, in spades.

Dial up that spiritual thermostat and put some heat under the folks around you. At the same time, you want to exude an attitude that says to your friends, *I still value this relationship, so we're going to work through this thing together.* This is where genuine maturity makes its mark.

The apostle James explains your role as a loving brother this way:

But the wisdom that comes from heaven is first of all pure; then peace-loving, considerate, submissive, full of mercy and good fruit, impartial and sincere. *Peacemakers who sow in peace raise a harvest of righteousness.* (James 3:17–18)

I like that Scripture calls loving, considerate believers "peacemakers." But I want you to note something before you begin living your life of purity before the world. There's a nasty, blind fork in the road out there. If you lack the maturity to walk as a loving peacemaker, you may end up taking the wrong turn, and your heart of love for your brother might collapse. Let's look again at the Scripture verse I placed at the beginning of this chapter:

> Make every effort to live in peace with all men and to be holy; without holiness no one will see the Lord. See to it that no one misses the grace of God and that *no bitter root grows up to cause trouble and defile many.* (Hebrews 12:14–15)

"Make every effort to live in peace with all men and to be holy"? Okay, this refers to peacefully pressing through relational conflicts so that no one can miss seeing His grace. That's clear enough. But what do bitter roots have to do with all this? How strange that our Father should follow up this command to holiness with a warning about bad attitudes!

It gets stranger still when you notice what verses precede His command to avoid every hint of sexual immorality (see Ephesians 5:3):

> Get rid of all bitterness, rage and anger, brawling and slander, along with every form of malice. Be kind and compassionate to one another, forgiving each other, just as in Christ God forgave you. (Ephesians 4:31–32)

I doubt this happened by coincidence, because our Father understands the human heart so well. Let's go back to Ben's story from chapter 6:

> I just can't deal with all the un-Christlike Christians around me any-more. My defenses are getting weak, and I'm afraid that I'll use Michelle sexually in the near future. No one close to me wants to walk

in integrity: they keep the parts of the Bible they like and toss out the parts they don't. They say things like, "God didn't specifically say anything about that, so it must be all right to do it."

I'm tired of the burdens and the anxiety, tired of the late nights mulling this over and over and over in my head. I fear for my soul and for the souls of those around me. I fear for my relationship with Michelle because I very much want her to be better off for having known me (as you said in *Every Young Man's Battle*), but I'm afraid that with my resolve crumbling, I'll end up grabbing her chest.

I fear for my relationship with God, because with all the Christians around me ignoring Him and doing whatever they want, it is getting harder and harder for me to believe in Him.

Ben's angry. He's confused and discouraged, and though he's surrounded himself with Christians, he feels disconnected from nearly all of them. Anger and bitterness are always dangerous to your walk with God because they disconnect you from others and cut you off from His river of peace.

You need to understand this connection between purity and bitterness if you expect to answer God's challenge to love your brother as yourself. As paradoxical as it may seem, a radical touch from God can quickly nudge you over the precipice of bitterness. You start out with such loving motives. You've seen God's truth clearly, and you can't help being excited. God's touch has taken you to a deeper level of connection and peace with Him, and you now know so well what your friends desperately need to know. You want to shout it to the world so that everyone can experience it with you.

When the relational earthquakes commence, you remain an undaunted warrior, doggedly pressing through relational conflicts. You're sure that everyone will hear exactly what you've heard from God—if they will just listen. Over time they finally accept the pure, new you as a permanent change.

The trouble is, they haven't listened well enough to change along with you. You're now the odd man out, stuck with paying a pricey social tab, and it's right here in the aftermath of those rolling earthquakes that your cagey Enemy whispers this thought in your mind: *Let them have it with both barrels! You're angry, right?*

I'm sure my son Jasen thought about giving those who teased him a piece of his mind, but he never did. He's kept the right, loving attitude toward such brothers throughout his years in high school and college.

As for myself, I was rather ticked at his friends, as well as those popular Christian kids in my daughter Laura's youth group. They crushed her spirit and made her feel miserable for two years because they wouldn't listen. Then my second daughter, Rebecca, took a similar emotional beating from that same youth group when one of her best friends was sexually victimized by the pastor. You don't think I was spitting mad after that happened?

I prayed many times with Rebecca as she struggled desperately to beat back the bitterness, and I watched her collapse into tears each time she begged God for release from her pain and anger. The experience ripped my heart out, and as I stewed over the fact that my own brothers in Christ were wreaking the havoc, I'm sure my bitterness bordered on hatred at times.

In the end, my bitter root grew to the thickness of a giant redwood tree. One Sunday afternoon Brenda was sitting in the La-Z-Boy in our master bedroom while I, sprawled across the bed, was grumbling again. I launched into a vitriolic rampage, listing name after name of my brothers at church and spewing angry lava about how each one had dropped their standards and left our girls in such a lurch.

As I ended my hot soliloquy, my eyes met Brenda's, and we both knew what the other was thinking. "Sweetheart," I said, "I just can't live with this bitterness anymore. I have got to find a way out of this, or it'll kill me. Will you pray with me right now?"

Brenda flipped a CD into the player, and we entered into worship together on the spot. Halfway through the first song, the Father spoke by bringing a favorite scripture to my mind—the same one He used on that glorious, starry night in Colorado when He set me free from the pain and scars from my relationship with my dad:

Here I am! I stand at the door and knock. If anyone hears my voice
and opens the door, I will come in and eat with him, and he with me.
(Revelation 3:20)

I love it when You knock on my door, Lord, my heart whispered back to
Him.

He didn't answer audibly, but I heard Him answer just the same. *And I
love to knock on your door. You answer quickly whenever I do, and I can always
count on taking you to the next place we need to go together. But you are getting
so angry at your brothers when they don't answer those same doors!*

But they are so hard hearted, Lord! I pressed.

*Would you get this angry if Dan didn't get up to answer your knock on his
door?*

Instantly my heart was stricken. Dan was a dear family friend, and he'd
been in a wheelchair and in constant pain for ten long years after falling thirty
feet from a bridge. I knew exactly what the Lord was getting at. Dan couldn't
stand up and walk to the door, no matter how long I knocked on it.

Many of your brothers can't answer their doors, either, He continued. *Some
are in constant pain, and they can't hear My knocking. Some hear Me, but they
just don't have the courage to go where I want to take them. Others are so confused
by their past that they can't even find their way to the next door.*

I thought about some of the things men have confessed to me about their
past. As I pondered those things, I understood completely what the Lord was
telling me. It's not always that guys *won't* answer the door to Him. It's more
like they *can't find* what it takes inside to answer Him yet.

That insight had never occurred to me before, and my heart began to
melt. I'd been horribly wrong and arrogant in my outlook.

*I desire to move forward with you as long as you keep answering My knock on
your door,* He said. *But I also want you to know that I'll be staying behind with
your brothers for as long as it takes them to answer too. You have to let go of their
responses to My knock on their door. That's My responsibility, and I take it on
gladly. While they may not be able to answer their door yet, I'll keep on knocking*

and keep on ministering to them until they have the faith and courage to open up to Me too. I long for their fainting hearts as much as I cherish your faithful one.

What could I say? What more could I do but drop my hands to my sides and give Him my heart once more? I thought He was finished, so I prepared to thank Him profusely in song. But just then, He leaned back into the room and whispered once more: *You need to know one more thing. I won't be able to keep knocking on new doors for you if every time I take you deeper, you just get angrier at your brothers who won't follow with you. Don't forget this.*

I was frozen by His words. Then He reminded me of another scripture that He'd taught me long ago:

> Whoever believes that Jesus is the Christ is born of God, and whoever loves the Father loves *the child born of Him.* (1 John 5:1, NASB)

Finally He left me with these kind words: *I will do nothing in your life that will weaken your love for your brothers, even if I have to stop knocking at your door and leave you right where you are spiritually. I love you too much to do otherwise.*

Message sent, and message delivered, loud and clear. We must walk in the truth, but we must always love our brothers as we do so. We must take our eyes off their responses and keep them fixed upon our own race at all times.

As you love your brothers by living faithfully before them as a sexually pure man, you know that the goal of this game is to draw them along with you into purity. But that goal must not be your focus. That's His focus. Your focus must be kept on the race and the joy of running.

You aren't responsible for how they receive that love or whether they answer His knock on their door. Love your brothers, and above all, get into your journey. Throw your whole heart into the race, because no one can ever take those moments away from you:

> Real wisdom, God's wisdom, begins with a holy life and is character-
> ized by getting along with others. It is gentle and reasonable, overflow-

ing with mercy and blessings, not hot one day and cold the next, not two-faced. You can develop a healthy, robust community that lives right with God and enjoy its results only if you do the hard work of getting along with each other, treating each other with dignity and honor. (James 3:17–18, MSG)

For Personal Reflection

1. Think back to a relational aftershock that you've experienced as a result of taking a step toward God. Did you press through on the changes or back off?
2. What is the reward for enduring these relational conflicts?
3. Why does bitterness often follow a radical touch from God?

17

Granting Room

Holy Father, protect them by the power
of your name—the name you gave me—so that
they may be one as we are one.

—JOHN 17:11

My friend Dave is a real hero of the faith when it comes to every man's battle. When I explained what God had planned for this final section of *Tactics*, excitement rose in his voice. "I love the concept of brothers defending and protecting each other," he said. "The Enemy has been very successful in dividing us in this battle. We have to hide our weaknesses and fight on our own way too often."

Then Dave turned even more passionate. "We are at war! We must bind together. That was Jesus's prayer for us, that we would be one as He and the Father are one. There's strength in unity, but we're letting the Enemy keep us apart."

One of the major areas of *disunity* among Christian brothers is the topic of personal convictions. Such convictions normally arrive by special delivery, courtesy of the Holy Spirit, and He wasted no time delivering mine. The "Big One" arrived shortly after I'd pulled up stakes in California and headed back to Iowa. It happened while I was visiting my family in Cedar Rapids and I decided to bop into the Stage 4 Theaters one warm summer evening to catch a new movie.

I always loved going to the movies. Something about the way films transport you to another world had fascinated me ever since I was a young kid. On this particular evening, I was enjoying the movie immensely until the hero fell asleep. He immediately entered into a dream, and the screen dissolved into a dream sequence of grotesque, blasphemous images. I'm talking about blood being splattered all over the place on things I held dear—lambs, crosses, and other spiritual images. To this day, I'm not quite sure what statement the filmmaker was trying to make about Christianity.

All I know is that I suddenly "heard" this piercing, tortured scream in my spirit in response to those brutal images on screen. I quickly stood up and quietly walked out of the show, not sure exactly why I was leaving but absolutely certain I should. I couldn't have been more than two steps past the theater entrance when I heard the Holy Spirit command, *You will no longer go to theaters.*

I didn't argue. There was nothing to argue about. "You got it," I said as I walked straight to my car.

Does that story sound weird to you? It probably does, which is why I'm probably risking more by telling you about this theater incident than by describing my days of chasing women and flipping through skin magazines. But what I heard that evening was a direct, personal request by my Father.

I haven't darkened the door of a movie theater since that incident twenty-five years ago. I'm sure the next thing you're wondering is whether I watch *any* movies. I can assure you that I enjoy watching videos at home with Brenda and the family, and I have the largest collection of old television shows and Hollywood movies of anyone on my block—probably more than a thousand titles, with many in DVD. I have nothing against movies, and neither does God, as long as they are clean (and as you might imagine, mine are).

But I know my Father has asked me not to step inside movie theaters anymore. I don't really know why. Perhaps the Lord knew it would help me win my battle for sexual purity more quickly and, in time, prepare me to write books on that topic. Perhaps the Lord has big spiritual plans for one of my sons, and the hot previews shown at the theaters might one day trigger a sexual sin that would derail the Lord's plan for him. In any event, the reasons didn't matter to me, and I've spent little time dwelling on them over the years. He is my Father, and He has the right to make personal requests of me. I suppose that is why we call these *personal* convictions.

Something like not going to the movies shouldn't become *your* conviction unless God has personally impressed upon you to make that sacrifice. God doesn't expect you to run *my* race or adopt *my* standards. He only expects you to make room for them—and for me—in the body of Christ. In other words, you don't have to give up going to movie theaters to have unity with me. I only need to be free to run the way God has asked me to run, *with* perseverance and *without* penalty from my brothers and sisters in Christ.

Hard to Obey

When it comes to these differences between us, the apostle Paul gave us the following directions:

> Therefore let us stop passing judgment on one another. Instead, make up your mind not to put any stumbling block or obstacle in your brother's way. (Romans 14:13)

I know from painful experience that this is one verse many young men have a whale of a time obeying, because I've been judged plenty for my conviction about theaters. I've been told I'm legalistic, out of touch, and too unrealistic for today's culture.

Here's an example. In my hometown, my kids' youth group divides into small groups on Sunday nights for relationship building and fun. One time, Keith, one of the lay leaders, called parents beforehand to let them know he was planning to show the group a PG-13 movie. He made the round of phone calls to make room for the personal convictions of the parents, which was commendable.

But when a father objected to the movie, Keith said this at the next leaders' meeting: "Parents who don't let their kids watch movies like this are *so* anal!" He was scornful as the others laughed.

I wasn't at the meeting, but when I heard about what Keith had said, I was hurt and offended, because what he said meant *my* convictions are rigid too.

In Romans 14, Paul said such behavior is unloving and breaks down unity among brothers. And you know what? Paul was right. I felt trashed and marginalized by everyone who laughed at that meeting.

When it comes to the battle for sexual purity, the stakes are too high for any of us to make snide or belittling comments. Keith's jab nicked me pretty good, and it's common for other people's insensitive comments about another's *personal* convictions to result in disharmony and disunity.

If you're going to be a loving brother and carry someone else's burdens in this battle, you have to watch your attitudes regarding your brothers and their personal convictions, as this scripture points out:

> Bear (endure, carry) one another's burdens and troublesome moral faults, and in this way fulfill and observe perfectly the law of Christ (the Messiah) and complete what is lacking [in your obedience to it]. *For if any person thinks himself to be somebody [too important to condescend to shoulder another's load] when he is nobody [of superiority except in his own estimation], he deceives and deludes and cheats himself.* (Galatians 6:2–3, AMP)

Look again at the italicized lines. Keith got into trouble because he thought his "enlightened" and "sophisticated" understanding of grace and godliness allowed him to laugh at the legalistic brothers who just didn't get it.

Keith just "knew" that differing views about theaters had been born of old-fashioned, narrow-minded thinking. He was mistaken because he wasn't

God. He couldn't see into my heart or anyone else's heart and know the story behind our personal convictions.

Keith also assumed that the children of such parents must obviously chafe beneath the bondage of such parenting, but he was blind on that score too.

Sure, sticking to my guns on this issue brought some tension at home early on. When my daughter Laura was fourteen years old, she once called for a family conference to demand an explanation about "this theater thing." She explained that she'd been taking a lot of heat from her friends over the issue at church and school, so I thought her question was fair.

When Brenda and I pulled the four kids together and told them about my experiences years before at the Stage 4 Theaters, tears pooled in my eyes. "I know what your friends are saying," I said. "I know how hard this is for you too, but I can't justify giving you the money to go to theaters when God has clearly told me not to go myself. When you're in college, you'll be free to make up your own mind, and I won't say a word about your decision either way. But for now, I don't know what else to do. I've wrestled with this over and over again, but I just can't seem to find any other solution for you that still honors God. If you can help me find that solution, I'm open to it. I love you."

All four kids teared up as well. Silently, they all looked at one another. Finally Laura spoke up, "Daddy, it's hard, but we will stand with you in this." They did it because they love me, sure. But they did it mostly for their audience of One. He had asked them to obey their parents on this earth, and that was good enough for them.

As a parent, this was one of the greatest moments of my life, one I'll treasure forever.

Give the Benefit of the Doubt

During that family conference on movies there were no harsh rules, cross words, or subtle rebellion. We were just six people standing together and hanging in there with our Father's dreams. That's exactly God's point when He commands us to stop passing judgment on each other's convictions in Romans 14:13. We can't see into the hearts and lives of our brothers, no matter how enlightened and sophisticated we think we've become. If your brother thinks differently than you do, give him the benefit of the doubt.

That's why the apostle Peter insists that we humble ourselves in our relationships with each other:

> Finally, all of you, live in harmony with one another; be sympathetic,
> love as brothers, be compassionate and humble. (1 Peter 3:8)

If anyone ever *did* have the right to make fun of others, it would have been the apostle Paul, a man as enlightened in God's ways as anyone who's ever lived, besides Jesus Himself. But Paul taught us a better way to approach our differences than by making fun of them. When discussing what foods were okay to eat, Paul suggested in Romans that personal convictions and other disputable matters would be common within the Christian community:

> Accept him whose faith is weak, without passing judgment on dis-
> putable matters. One man's faith allows him to eat everything, but
> another man, whose faith is weak, eats only vegetables. The man who
> eats everything must not look down on him who does not, and the
> man who does not eat everything must not condemn the man who
> does, for God has accepted him. (Romans 14:1–3)

When Paul used the term *faith* here, he was not referring to saving faith in Christ but to confidence in one's liberty in Christ. In this case, "strong" Christians such as Paul understood that their diet had no spiritual significance. The "weak" simply were not yet clear as to the status of the Old Testament regulations under Christ's New Covenant.

Paul proclaimed that, for similar reasons, Christians won't agree on all matters pertaining to the Christian life—partly because God didn't address every matter in Scripture and partly because He's given each of us different personal convictions. But even in the midst of the differences, the motivations of the weak and the strong are generally the same—both want to avoid sin and to serve God fully. There simply is no room to judge from either position.

Because of this, unity among Christians can't be and shouldn't be based upon everyone's agreement on disputable questions. In other words, you don't have to agree with your brothers in order to maintain unity with them. You simply have to handle the differences lovingly by granting your brother the room he needs to live spiritually before his Father, and at your side. Paul teaches us to make room for a brother's belief rather than cut him away:

> Therefore let us stop passing judgment on one another. Instead, make up your mind not to put any stumbling block or obstacle in your brother's way. As one who is in the Lord Jesus, I am fully convinced that no food is unclean in itself. But...if your brother is distressed because of what you eat, you are no longer acting in love. Do not by your eating destroy your brother for whom Christ died....
>
> Let us therefore make every effort to do what leads to peace and to mutual edification. *Do not destroy the work of God* for the sake of food. All food is clean, but *it is wrong* for a man to eat anything that causes someone else to stumble. *It is better not to eat meat* or drink wine or to do anything else that will cause your brother to fall. (Romans 14:13–15, 19–21)

Paul was the leader of the Gentile church and had the power to decide such disagreements himself. He could have demanded that everyone believe his way regarding the meat sacrificed to idols. He could have ordered everyone to eat a nice slab of beef any time the brothers had a meal together to enforce unity. But while that would have ended the impasse on the surface, true group unity would have been dead on arrival, because every guy who considered eating sacrificial meat a sin would have been violating his conscience with every bite. When you don't allow your brother the room to maintain in his heart his clean standing before God, there can be no unity.

If you expect to maintain total unity in your own group today, your brother must be free to play out his life before his audience of One, without fear of ridicule and without the fear that you'll ice him socially. Otherwise you're tossing a stumbling block of laughter and derision before his faith and his intimacy with God.

Dealing with Differences

I can bring Paul's teaching a little closer to home if we dump the idol meat and replace it with differing convictions regarding media and film. Just like a conviction against sacrificial idol meat cramped Paul's meal planning in his day, my personal conviction about theaters would cramp your style if I were part of your gang. What will you do with me on Friday nights when everyone wants to hit the flicks? The natural way to deal with these differences is the world's way—you would simply cut me out of your plans for that evening and over time ease me out of the group, isolating me on the social fringe.

It's like those old high-school cliques, where if you don't think like the group, you can't belong. That's exactly what happened to my daughter Laura. Her movie standards were much tighter than those of a few of the more popular guys in the youth group, so they cut her off socially. To hang out with her friends, Laura either had to watch those PG-13 videos and violate her conscience or be eliminated from the group's weekend social calendar.

Paul would have been horrified to see Laura treated this way, and if we paraphrase Paul's words from Romans, we can guess how clearly he would have rebuked these guys: "Look, your entertainment choices shouldn't be your only focus. No Christian should live for himself alone, but rather for Christ's purposes. God called you to help carry your brothers' and sisters' burdens in this battle for purity. Why are you tormenting Laura in this way?"

He might have continued in this way: "Guys, you believe these PG and

PG-13 movies are okay, and you want to watch them. So what? If you force this issue when Laura is around, that hurts her, so you're no longer walking according to love. Don't make her change or have to break away from the group! Aren't you willing to quit watching these on the nights she's around rather than hurt God's work among you?"

Paul went on to say:

> Do not allow what you consider good to be spoken of as evil. For the
> kingdom of God is not a matter of eating and drinking [or getting
> your way in all the entertainment choices], but of righteousness, peace
> and joy in the Holy Spirit, because anyone who serves Christ in this
> way is pleasing to God and approved by men. (Romans 14:16–18)

Paul was willing to stop eating "unclean" food rather than hurt his brother in Christ. If these guys in Laura's youth group had chosen Paul's way of handling differences, they could have pleased God, and it wouldn't have cost them much. To follow God and to maintain unity with Laura, all they had to do was once in a while watch a few videos with a slower pace and more romance and character development and fewer sexual innuendos than their usual slam-bam fare.

It's sad to admit this, but the only young men I've seen handle a situation similar to Laura's in a normal Christian way—or Paul's way—was a group of mostly *non*-Christian guys that Jasen hung out with in high school.

These truly humble guys didn't think too highly of themselves. I've often marveled at the level of maturity they displayed in handling their differences with Jasen, and I've wondered how they got there. I'm sure it didn't happen this way, but I could imagine these friends holding a meeting regarding Jasen's "membership" in their group.

Pounding his gavel, the chairman droned, "I now bring this meeting to order! As our first order of business, who now speaks in favor of admitting Jasen into our group?"

"Well, ya gotta love Jasen. He's a cold-blooded assassin in paintball!" Dan declared.

"Yeah, and he loves racing ATVs," Nick added. "And don't forget his WWII vintage military rifle from Yugoslavia. That's really cool to shoot."

"He's the absolute king of video games," Tim chipped in. "We've all taken a beating at his hands." Everyone moaned along with him for a moment before breaking into the laughter of appreciation.

"His car is no better than any of ours, and that's a plus!" Seth added to more laughter.

Everything was looking great for Jasen until the chairman broke in again. "But he doesn't go to movie theaters!"

"Hey, Jasen is cool," Dan retorted. "We'll work around that."

We'll work around that. How novel! And amazingly enough, that's what these guys did. If they decided to hit the movies on a Friday night, they never dreamed of icing Jasen for the entire evening. They'd go to the show, but as soon as the movie was over, they'd call on their cells and say, "Hey, meet us at Seth's in ten minutes, bro. And be prepared to die; it's Nintendo time!"

I was excited to see this kind of loving action among the non-Christians at Jasen's high school, but I sure wish I'd have found more of it in the church along the way. A couple of verses pop into my mind:

Many a man claims to have unfailing love,
   but a faithful man who can find? (Proverbs 20:6)

Dear children, let us not love with words or tongue but with actions
and in truth. (1 John 3:18)

Jasen's non-Christian friends made it a lot easier for him with his audience of One. Laura's youth group "friends" made it a lot tougher. If you expect to be a great man of God, you must decide to become a faithful man who loves in action.

It's right here where you can make a real mark on the spiritual front of purity's battle. Are you willing to free your brother to run the race marked out for him *without* penalty from the body of Christ? Are you mature enough to handle the differences within your group?

I urge you to form community with your brothers in spite of your differences. Your very character as a Christian teammate is riding upon it, as well as the overall sexual purity of the body of Christ.

Fight for what's right. Be bigger than your own crew, and make sure that connection is happening for everyone around you. Bring others from the social fringes back to center.

Helping others live at peace with who they are in God is a great work. Be a hero. It's part of loving your brother as yourself.

For Personal Reflection

1. Have you ever received a direct, personal request from your Father? Do you understand why He gave you this personal conviction?
2. What price have you paid for this conviction? What has this done in your attitudes toward others?
3. If we don't have the same convictions, can we still have unity?
4. Will sacrifice always play a part in maintaining unity?
5. Ponder again these questions from the top of this page: Are you willing to free your brother to run the race marked out for him *without* penalty from the body of Christ? Are you mature enough to handle these differences lovingly within your group?

No Brother Left Behind

We challenge you to stop ridiculing your friends
who are trying to walk closer to God.

—*EVERY YOUNG MAN'S BATTLE*

A s a young man, you have to accept your deep need for intimacy if you expect victory over sexual sin. You aren't a rock; you aren't an island. God has made it perfectly clear from the beginning of time that it's not good for man to be alone. You must accept your need for intimacy if you expect to win this battle, just as Allen is beginning to understand:

> There is a pervasive loneliness that I'm feeling throughout my life. I
> think that most of this has to do with me still trying to hide who I
> really am with others. I'm realizing that I have been trying to live my
> life completely alone for some time, and my track record isn't too good.

Almost all of us have lousy track records when we *live* alone, and now that you understand your sexual vulnerabilities as a guy, it should be clear why it isn't wise to *fight* this battle alone, either. Teaming up with a few good men to fight for a shared purpose can really carry the day in purity's battle, and to be honest, it doesn't even have to be a *spiritual* purpose. Any kind of shared purpose may do the trick, as long as it delivers genuine connection. That's the way it went for Nate:

> During the summer after my freshman year, I spent a lot of time in the weightroom with my teammates as we prepared for the football season. I went seven months without masturbating, and I thought I finally had this under control. But when football ended, I had a lot of time on my hands alone, and I couldn't fight it anymore.

Real intimacy packs a punch in the battle for any guy. If the shared purpose is the battle for sexual purity, it's that much better, as Gordon attests:

> Several years ago I spent two years hooked on soft-core porn. I finally broke free after realizing what a wretched person I had become; I couldn't stand the way I viewed women anymore. But even after I broke that habit, another habit persisted. For roughly eight more years, I masturbated regularly. I knew it was hurting me, but I was completely hooked.
>
> Finally several of my college friends admitted they were in the same battle, so we decided to break our habits together. I found that having a large group of strong Christian friends and the daily accountability of a roommate helped me out immensely. I have not masturbated for over three months now, and I'm feeling stronger all the time.

If you feel connected and accepted by those around you, you'll have plenty of true intimacy in your life, and you won't need the false intimacy of pornography and masturbation to make up for what's missing. That's why the encouragement of your brothers and sisters in Christ is so vital. It's why God expects you to take responsibility for your actions and how they affect your connection with other Christian guys.

Dismissing loneliness as an obstacle to purity can be easy. And perhaps you think you don't need to get connected, because you don't see the value of a Christian brother standing with you in this fight. If so, let me remind you that no matter how strong your internal defenses are, there's a weak spot in your sexuality that's vulnerable to attack: disconnection.

Eric was a college student living with some Christian friends who all decided to fight this battle together. They talked often and prayed for each other regularly for eight months. After a friend prayed for him one night, Eric sensed God saying to him, "You aren't going to do that anymore." I'll let Eric continue his story:

> From that point on, I stopped masturbating. It was like God had dried up my sex drive, but it was more than that. He had truly given me the self-discipline to push all impure thoughts out of my mind. Whenever the Enemy attacked, God was right there and gave me the strength to stand. I went on like that for almost a year.
>
> But then I got a girlfriend, and I started masturbating again because I got so turned on when I was with her. We didn't do a lot physically—only kissed for the first year and a half—but still I'd get turned on being with her and end up masturbating when I got home.
>
> After all this, I was back right where I started—masturbating regularly—but in the back of my mind, I thought I could quit at any time because God had delivered me at one time. I was fooling only myself, though. Before long, my girlfriend and I started going further and further sexually, and after about two and a half years, we started having intercourse. That was the beginning of the end. We broke up after three and a half years.
>
> Needless to say, it has been very difficult to get back on the purity track since then. It has now been more than three years since I broke up with her, and I'm long out of college. To get back on track, I'm trying to reconnect and build true accountability with a new group of guys, because I've found that without that connection it's tough to get any sense of self-control. I feel I have the same mind-set as I did in my college days, but the main difference is that I had amazing accountability back then. I need that today.

Did you notice how easy it was for Eric to slip away when genuine intimacy with his brothers was compromised? Maybe you think you don't need the peer pressure from accountability groups to help you stand purely. Well, perhaps you don't. I didn't.

But even if you don't need the peer pressure, I assure you that you do need the *genuine intimacy* of friendship and acceptance. That is what creates the defensive perimeter for your sexual vulnerability, and every man needs that in his life, no matter who he is.

Interpersonal relationships are so potent that they can practically break the power of the masturbation cycle on their own. Sean told me that a simple decision to reach out to another guy made all the difference for him:

> I woke up one morning and realized that I was letting the world slip by because of all the hours I was wasting with my cyber-girls. I decided I wasn't going to look at porn or masturbate any longer, so I called my friend Rich and asked him to be my accountability partner. I went out and bought *Every Young Man's Battle,* and I've already gone four weeks without the porn and masturbation.
>
> I've started reading my Bible again, which I'd done little of since I was thirteen. I've also started praying, which I've never done regularly. My life has taken a definite upswing. I'm happy, I'm more peaceful, and I am easier to get along with. Rich and I have also added some guys to our accountability group, and we are discussing not only how to talk about all this, but how to take action when one of us falls.

A Band of Brothers

You aren't called to manage your lust on your own or to hide it from your brothers. You're to march out purposefully and kill the lust—together. Choose up teams and plan your schemes. Then gun it down.

You have a direct call to defend your brother's sexual vulnerabilities with everything you've got, just as you are called to defend your own:

Brothers, if someone is caught in a sin, you who are spiritual should restore him gently. But watch yourself, or you also may be tempted. *Carry each other's burdens, and in this way you will fulfill the law of Christ.* (Galatians 6:1–2)

Carrying your brothers' burdens is part of every Christian's destiny, and it's intriguing that the emphasis in the original language here is on *moral* burdens or weaknesses. In addition, the original Greek word for the verb *carry* is used elsewhere for "setting broken bones" and "bringing factions together." I find this fascinating. When I ponder this verse in the context of setting broken bones, I'm reminded how much this verse is like the one I used in introducing this section of the book:

Therefore, strengthen your feeble arms and weak knees. "Make level paths for your feet," so that the lame may not be disabled, but rather healed. (Hebrews 12:12–13)

In both cases, God is reminding you to be diligent in tending to your restoration so that you can be equally diligent in working on your brothers' behalf. But when I ponder this verse in the context of bringing factions together, I also remember why my Father intertwines my destiny with His. As His obedient son, He hopes that my faithful example will restore my brothers back to normal so we can all live peacefully in a healthy, flourishing family.

The need for restoration is everywhere. Many of our brothers are swamped by pain, though most guys keep their desperation well hidden. For instance, Kevin has been blasted below the waterline by the torpedoes of his past, but who would know it? He's a rising star, a successful twenty-something with a PhD, but while he's blazing a wide swath in the business world, his insides have been burned beyond recognition by the past traumas of home, high school, and college.

While Kevin's story is long, I use it here to remind you that your brothers

are aching, whether you know it or not. They need someone—anyone—to
toss them a lifeline of intimacy:

> Last night my friend Steve called and asked me to get up early to pray
> with him at 6:45 a.m. I told him, "Sorry, buddy. Saturday is my only
> day to sleep in." He persisted, so I finally told him I'd think about it.
>
> When we hung up, I fell asleep on my futon with the television
> on, and the next thing I knew it was about midnight and my room-
> mate was heading off to bed. I was very premeditated about what I did
> next. I aimed the remote at the TV and hopped from one channel to
> another, hoping to find something racy on one of the movie channels.
> At that late hour, HBO and Showtime did not disappoint me.
>
> Part of me wanted badly to do the mature thing and to go to bed
> so I could get up and meet Steve, but the rest of me wanted nothing
> more than to watch soft porn all night. The movie channels won the
> day—I mean evening—and when I finally went to bed, it was around
> four-thirty in the morning. I felt ashamed, exhausted, and guilty as I
> crawled into bed. I fell asleep pretty quickly, but I was soon awakened
> by the ring tones of my cell phone.
>
> I knew it was Steve, but I let it go to voice mail because I had been
> sleeping for only two hours when he called. I finally got up around
> nine and called him back. Of course, he reminded me I had missed the
> prayer thing, but he also said that he was going to meet a few of the
> gang at the health club. "We're going to play some hoops around
> 11:00. I hope you can join us," he said.
>
> Steve knows my struggle with porn and masturbation, and I think
> he could tell something was wrong by the sound of my voice, so before
> we hung up, he insisted, "Don't miss this, Kevin. Be there, okay?"
>
> "Okay, I'll see you at 11:00, Steve," I replied. I headed off to the
> shower to get ready when the computer called out my name. I mean, it
> was almost audible, the voice was so strong, and before long, I was lost
> in some porn sites until 10:35. Ugh! I still had to take a shower and

drive halfway across the city to meet them at 11:00. The bottom line: I wasn't going to make it on time. Still, I jumped into the shower to try to make it anyway when suddenly I felt emotionally and physically awful.

I sat down on my futon and flipped on the TV to some football game, and for the next two hours, I stared at the television, although I didn't really watch it. I just sat there motionless, verbally pounding myself: *You are so worthless. They wouldn't want to hang out with you anyway. Your life stinks. You are a waste! You don't even have anyone to call about this. You're such a loser!*

I've heard myself say those same things many times before. I finally shouted at myself, *Kevin, you used to be so friendly and energetic, so caring toward people. Now you don't care!*

Then I started crying hard, and I can't begin to express how much anger, frustration, shame, and self-loathing I felt at that moment.... I kept shouting to myself, *You created all of these walls, Kevin! People aren't going to hurt you!*

I only wish I could believe that last one. Many people have hurt me, including my family. My father was so aloof, and he has never accepted me to this day. My resulting fear of people and [my] social isolation always work to keep me in my place. That's what all the popular kids in elementary school used to tell me: "You need to stay in your place, Kevin!" They wanted me to stay a loser.

But I am not a loser! This hurts so much. Look at all the accomplishments in my life—from college and grad school—and the really nice job I have, and yet I still feel like that loser back in third grade. They got me, Fred. My dad won, and those kids won. I may have a graduate degree on the wall that proves I'm not a loser, but they still got me.

Kevin's story resonated deeply with me. Just like Kevin, I remember not showing up for my friends for all sorts of angst-ridden reasons. I haven't forgotten the times I pounded myself endlessly with lines like *They don't really like me* or *They'll have more fun without me* or *I don't fit in with them anyway.*

I remember vividly the loneliness and the pain of confusion, of wondering who I was and if anyone really cared about me. I needed a warrior like Steve to save the day, someone who wouldn't stop pulling me out of my shell—someone who would pull me toward Jesus.

Consider our command in Galatians once more, but this time from *The Message:*

> *Live creatively, friends.* If someone falls into sin, forgivingly restore him, saving your critical comments for yourself. You might be needing forgiveness before the day's out. (Galatians 6:1, MSG)

"Live creatively, friends." I love that phrase. We're made to live that way. But too often we spend our creative energy avoiding obedience and dancing at the edges of God's ways because we're afraid we'll miss out on a good time. How misguided. If we'd just throw our full heart behind our brothers, we'd launch our full creativity into their emotional chaos and embark on the adventure of a lifetime. We'd become shining stars in the midst of a dark universe, pointing men back to the center. A normal, healthy, and flourishing family portrait would result, if Randy's story is any indication:

> I'm in college now, but when I was a sophomore in high school, my church replaced Wednesday-night sermons with discipleship groups. We had tried these D-groups before, but they never lasted. This time they did, however.
>
> My group had seven guys and a youth leader named Andy. When we met the first week, Andy asked us what we wanted to study for the next semester, and one guy jokingly answered, "Sex"!
>
> Andy laughed like the rest of us, but he took that as his cue to suggest that we study *Every Young Man's Battle.* He ordered eight copies, and we all began to read your book. Once we came to the section on

masturbation, we decided we should do more than study this issue. We all agreed this was something we should tackle together.

We started out being accountable to each other by giving a recap of our previous week every time we met. The procedure was easy: Andy would ask us how the week had gone, and we'd signal with either a thumbs-up, meaning we had been clean, or a thumbs-down, meaning we had done the dirty deed. We soon came up with a clever name for this group of ours—the No Whack Pack.

For short, we called it the NWP. We kept our small group going all through high school, and we even tried to introduce our idea to other guys-only D-groups, but honestly, not everyone was up to the challenge.

My NWP group stuck it out to the end, and even though we've moved on to college or careers, we still talk all the time. We are the closest brothers you can imagine. Even when we are in separate corners of the world, we know we're each praying for the others to stay pure. When we are all back in town over the holidays, we get together and go through our NWP procedure. If anyone is failing, we encourage him and offer tips we've learned from our own days on the battleground.

NWP has kept us close to God and His will for our lives. Because it is such a big part of our lives, we seek out ways to constantly remind ourselves of the pact we've joined. We recently took the Hebrew letters for "NWP" and created a symbol that makes a public display of the pact.

Wow. Talk about creativity. And talk about a healthy, flourishing branch in God's family!

A Great Description

Genuine intimacy is beautiful to behold, and Randy's story has the fragrance of Jesus all over it. I'm reminded of Isaiah's description of Christ's loving character and kingdom:

In love a throne will be established;
in faithfulness a man will sit on it—
    one from the house of David—
one who in judging seeks justice
    and speeds the cause of righteousness. (Isaiah 16:5)

I love that last phrase: "and speeds the cause of righteousness." This prompts me to come up with the perfect pop-quiz question for you: *Brother, does your current lifestyle speed the cause of righteousness in our family?* The men of NWP—your brothers—are setting an awesome example for the rest of the family.

What a ministry they have, right in their own backyard, and all they had to do was step up and choose to complete what was lacking in their lives:

Bear (endure, carry) one another's burdens and troublesome moral
faults, and in this way fulfill and observe perfectly the law of Christ
(the Messiah) and complete what is lacking [in your obedience to it].
(Galatians 6:2, AMP)

If you haven't started already, you should be praying intently for God's will for your future. I have a young friend in medical school who is looking forward to using his skills to heal the crippled and sick and dying on overseas mission trips. That's pretty cool. Maybe you're hoping your Father will give you a similar noble mission.

Well, don't look now, but He already has. He's calling you to set the broken bones and to heal the lame today, right where you live or go to school. I know of a college campus where students began discussion groups around *Every Young Man's Battle* and formed accountability groups so they could stand together. They didn't run from God's call to purity. They embraced it and threw their full creativity into it, just like the warriors of NWP. I shared their story in *Every Man's Challenge*, but since that book was aimed at married men, I want to share it again here:

One group of guys developed a plan to help each one stop masturbating. Each person picked a day of the week to masturbate, and that was the only day he could do it. If you missed your day, you had to wait until the next week. Once you had developed this measure of control, you moved it up a notch and picked one day every two weeks as your day of masturbation.

As it turned out, by the time the group was ready to notch it up to once every three weeks, they all agreed that the exercise had become silly and unnecessary. Each had formed so much control over their sexuality that they no longer needed a day of masturbation.

Professors told me of young men, trapped in compulsive masturbation for years, who found complete freedom as openness and accountability robbed the habit of its power to dominate their lives. Guys who had been quite reserved came out of their shells and began to connect with others in new ways. And as word of this group's victory spread, more groups grew and more young men who had felt alienated from God began to experience a connection with Him they had never known. They were all using the right weapons, fighting the battle together and finding victory together. The word *together* is the key word. If we are vulnerable and open to taking a risk with our brothers, we are never doomed to fail or to live a life of loneliness and isolation.

As you know by now, when I was a starting quarterback on my high-school team, I was consumed by football. We were the second-largest high school in the state, so we had a big pool of athletes. The Jefferson High J-Hawk football team was loaded with natural athletes who could really bring it on Friday nights.

But three guys stood above the rest in my mind, and they were my three mighty men—center Dave Millis, left guard Duane Poole, and fullback Bruce Feuerhelm. If I came to a third-and-two on tense, autumn nights, I'd ram a hand-off into Bruce's midsection and send him hurtling through the hole between Dave and Duane. Few could stop that play, because all three of my mighty men were involved at the point of attack.

They were just as committed to football as I was, and they didn't just bring their A-game to every practice and game. They also had integrity, men who were as faithful in life as they were in pads. I could have left my girlfriend with any one of them in a hotel room some night and not lost a bit of sleep. Were they Christians? No. But they were more trustworthy than many Christian guys I knew. Why? Because we were teammates, and that was all they needed to know.

What about you? Is your commitment to God's purposes just as deep, just as true? I challenge you to shoulder your responsibility to purity on one side and to help carry your brother's burden on the other. Your integrity rests on it, as well as your intimacy with Christ. Don't be satisfied to simply *seem* like a mighty man of God. Rise up and *be* a mighty man of God. Don't settle for being cool. Be pure.

Playing high-school football was fun, but Friday nights and touchdowns don't mean much in the long-distance race of faith. Carrying your brother's burden and being trusted by God as His warrior do.

Heroes of the Faith

Together, we can all become heroes, commended in Scripture for our faithful obedience:

> Others were tortured and refused to be released, so that they might gain a better resurrection. Some faced jeers and flogging, while still others were chained and put in prison. They were stoned; they were sawed in two; they were put to death by the sword. They went about in sheepskins and goatskins, destitute, persecuted and mistreated—*the world was not worthy of them.* They wandered in deserts and mountains, and in caves and holes in the ground.
>
> These were all commended for their faith. (Hebrews 11:35–39)

Perhaps your dad didn't tell you a thing about sex, or maybe he wasn't around to help you understand what's worth pouring your life into. Well, you have a new Father, and now He's told you. A worthy life comes from being about His business and becoming a strong branch in His family tree. It comes in living a life of holiness and complete obedience, regardless of what happens, and drawing all men to Christ by your example. It comes in defending the faithful, back to back, so that in the end, having done all, you will all stand tall.

Live your life on that plane where "the world is not worthy" of you. You are to live a life worthy of Him alone, no matter what the world thinks. He is your audience of One.

I'd like to leave you with the same challenge we gave at the conclusion of *Every Young Man's Battle:*

> We challenge you to live without premarital sex. We challenge you to live without masturbation. We challenge you to clean up what you're watching and the thoughts you're thinking.
>
> We challenge you to stop ridiculing your friends who are trying to walk closer to God. We challenge you to let the girls in your life know that you care more about their hearts than their bodies.

Other young warriors are rising up to these challenges to become heroes of the faith. Rise up and be one yourself. Commit to your Father's will, starting with your sexuality:

> God wants you to live a pure life.
>
> Keep yourselves from sexual promiscuity.
>
> Learn to appreciate and give dignity to your body, not abusing it, as is so common among those who know nothing of God. (1 Thessalonians 4:3–5, MSG)

Embrace this with all of your heart. Sure, guarding your heart and body may seem like a small thing in the ultimate scheme of God's kingdom, especially when compared to your brothers who were tortured, stoned, or sawed in two.

But do not despise the day of small beginnings. Do His will in the small things, and He will split the Jordan River before you, sweeping you into that promised land where you can live a fruitful life worthy of your Father and King.

Joy will bubble in His heart as you intertwine your destiny with His, and you will be mesmerized by the blessings pouring out of His delight in you.

Finally, this is my prayer for you: *May your heart be soft and your spine like steel, and may your faith be ever commended by Him.*

Now, go out and get it done, brother. Own the field. Make your Father proud.

For Personal Reflection

1. Ponder again this question from page 238: Brother, does your current lifestyle speed the cause of righteousness in our family tree? If you answer yes, would you be willing to ask a few brothers if they agree with you?

2. Explain how you're actively helping to set the bones of the brothers around you.

3. Is your commitment to carrying your brother's burden as strong as your commitment to carrying your own?

4. Are you willing to rise to the challenge of becoming a hero of the faith in regard to your brothers?

For Further Help

A good resource for questions about specific issues related to sexual addiction or abuse (or for counseling on any related problems) is New Life Ministries at www.newlife.com. They have many resources available and can suggest Christian counselors in your area that you could meet with. They also offer an online Sexual Purity Workshop for teens—a thirty-day program of fifteen streaming-video sessions and self-study workbook exercises that includes a thirty-minute coaching session, by phone, with a New Life personal coach. See site for details.

Notes

Chapter 1: Searching for the Merle Hay Moment

page

4 *"God's love is not based"*: Stephen Arterburn, Fred Stoeker, with Mike Yorkey, *Every Young Man's Battle* (Colorado Springs: Water-Brook, 2002), 20.

4 *"I recall how the Holy Spirit"*: Arterburn, Stoeker, Yorkey, *Every Young Man's Battle*, 20.

5 *"We must choose oneness"*: Arterburn, Stoeker, Yorkey, *Every Young Man's Battle*, 21–22.

Chapter 3: Eye Damage

39 *"[Porn] is a very carefully designed"*: Testimony, U.S. Senate Committee on Commerce, Science, and Transportation, November 18, 2004.

43 *"Sexual addicts develop tolerance"*: Mary Anne Layden, PhD, testimony, U.S. Senate Committee on Commerce, Science, and Transportation, November 18, 2004. Dr. Layden is the codirector of the Sexual Trauma and Psychopathology Program and director of education for the Center for Cognitive Therapy, Department of Psychiatry, University of Pennsylvania.

45 *"Girls…are waiting for Derek Jeter"*: David Amsden, "Not Tonight, Honey. I'm Logging On," http://newyorkmetro.com/nymetro/news/trends/n_9349/. Originally appeared in *New York Magazine*, October 20, 2003.

Chapter 4: Back to the Future

54 *"mature enough to watch"*: Stephen Arterburn and Shannon Ethridge, *Every Woman's Battle* (Colorado Springs: WaterBrook, 2003), 34.

Chapter 12: A Father's Trust

149 *"I feel incredible security":* Stephen Arterburn, Fred Stoeker, Brenda Stoeker, with Mike Yorkey, *Every Heart Restored* (Colorado Springs: WaterBrook, 2004), 189.

Chapter 13: Experiencing the Father in Prayer

160 "I used to get lustful thoughts": Arterburn, Stoeker, Yorkey, *Every Young Man's Battle,* 179.

163 *"When I graduated out of Teen Challenge":* From a sermon by Pastor Dave Olson, Heartland Church, Ankeny, Iowa, September 17, 2005. Used by permission.

165 *"All God's revelations":* Oswald Chambers, *My Utmost for His Highest* (Uhrichsville, OH: Barbour, 1935), October 10.

Chapter 14: Experiencing the Father Through Worship

184 *"Praise is God's sunlight":* Smith Wigglesworth, *The Complete Collection of His Life Teachings,* comp. Roberts Liardon (Tulsa: Albury, 1997), 839.

Chapter 18: No Brother Left Behind

239 "One group of guys": Stephen Arterburn, Fred Stoeker, with Mike Yorkey, *Every Man's Challenge: How Far Are You Willing to Go for God?* (Colorado Springs: WaterBrook, 2004), 50.

241 "We challenge you to live": Arterburn, Stoeker, Yorkey, *Every Young Man's Battle,* 214–15.